LIFE WORLD LIBRARY

ITALY

TIME INC. BOOK DIVISION

Editor   NORMAN P. ROSS
Art Director   LEONARD JOSSEL
Chief of Research   BEATRICE T. DOBIE

"Italy" was produced by the following editorial staff:

Editor, LIFE World Library   OLIVER E. ALLEN
Chief Researcher   GRACE BRYNOLSON
Researchers   DOROTHEA BOURNE, IRENE S. ERTUGRUL
JEAN SULZBERGER, RENÉE S. PICKEL
SHEILA OSMUNDSEN, LINDA ASHER
Picture Researchers   MARGARET K. GOLDSMITH
JOAN T. LYNCH
Art Associates   ALBERT J. DUNN, ROBERT L. YOUNG
Art Assistants   JAMES D. SMITH
JOHN M. WOODS, RICHARD FORTE
Copy Staff   MARIAN GORDON GOLDMAN
REBECCA CHAITIN, NORMA ROSEN, ANN SHAW
ANNE HUMPHERYS, DOLORES LITTLES
MARGARET RAMSAY

•

Publisher   JEROME S. HARDY
Production Staff   ROBERT E. FOY, JAMES P. MENTON
Circulation Staff   PHILIP E. JOHNSON, PETER KLOUTHIS
JOAN LANNING

•

LIFE MAGAZINE

Managing Editor   *Publisher*
EDWARD K. THOMPSON   C. D. JACKSON

•

The background text for this book was written by Herbert Kubly, the picture essays by Henry Moscow. The following individuals and departments of LIFE Magazine helped in producing the book: Ralph Crane, Loomis Dean, Eliot Elisofon, N. R. Farbman, Dmitri Kessel, Nina Leen, Walter Sanders and James Whitmore, staff photographers; Don Burke and the other Rome Bureau correspondents; Gene Farmer, Foreign News Editor; Ray Mackland, Picture Editor; George Caturani, Chief of the Foreign News Bureau; Doris O'Neil, Chief, LIFE Picture Library, and Content Peckham, Chief of the Time Inc. Bureau of Editorial Reference. Valuable help was also provided by Dora Jane Hamblin, former correspondent in the Rome Bureau.

LIFE WORLD LIBRARY

ITALY

by Herbert Kubly

and The Editors of LIFE

TIME INCORPORATED · NEW YORK · 1961

ABOUT THE WRITER

Herbert Kubly, born in Wisconsin, is of Swiss descent. He has been a newspaper reporter, art and music critic and playwright, and was at one time associate professor of speech at the University of Illinois.

In the text of this volume of the LIFE World Library, Mr. Kubly gives an interpretation of contemporary Italy drawn from his years of residence in the country, including a period of study as a Fulbright Fellow. From his experiences there, he has written two other books, *American in Italy* (National Book Award in 1956) and *Easter in Sicily*. His short stories with an Italian setting are collected in a third book, *Varieties of Love*.

OTHER BOOKS BY THE EDITORS OF LIFE:

LIFE's Picture History of World War II

LIFE's Picture History of Western Man

The World We Live In
  with Lincoln Barnett

The World's Great Religions

America's Arts and Skills

Picture Cook Book

The Second World War
  with Winston S. Churchill

The Wonders of Life on Earth
  with Lincoln Barnett

Contents

COVER: Variegated stucco houses line the quiet harbor of Portofino

Introduction

The introduction to any book about Italy can serve but one useful purpose: to remind the reader that the book itself can be only an introduction.

The debt of all our generations, past and living, to the source minds who have lived and died through the centuries on Italian soil has often been voiced. But even Italy, which has been fertility itself in the production of geniuses, has been unable to produce the historian-genius who could write a truly compendious history of the Italian peninsula with a comprehensive analysis of its impact on the science, art, religion, philosophy and government of mankind.

We who are not Italians, but who are nevertheless the heirs of the Mother Nation of men and cities, of laws and arts, do well to remind ourselves of our perennial debt. For the founding of the modern, independent Italian state took place just a hundred years ago.

The birth of Italy, which began with the *Risorgimento*, or "resurrection," was an event full of the hope of peace and the promise of progress for the new nation. But hope and promise were unhappily deferred by 80 years of economic struggle and many armed conflicts under the House of Savoy. The country, led to a most terrible defeat by Mussolini at the end of World War II, collapsed into catastrophic misery and poverty.

The "miracle of Italy"—to use the favorite phrase of foreigners—which began a decade ago is now the talk of all nations. This second *Risorgimento*, the cultural and economic resurrection of Italy, is almost without precedent in the annals of modern nations.

And yet it is not really a miracle. Nothing could be more natural, if we stop to remember that Italians *are* Italians.

Italy is poor in what men commonly call "raw materials," but it is uncommonly rich in the greatest raw material of all, human character. The gamut that the human mind, heart and soul can run is wider perhaps in Italy than in any other country. It is a land which since time out of mind has produced great saints and great sinners; geniuses and men of gigantic—and trivial—folly; heroes and knaves; champions of law, order and justice and black-hearted tyrants. (It is, therefore, one of the most likely countries in the West to "go Communist," but the least likely to bear the monolithic yoke of Communist leveling afterward.) All the "paradoxes" of modern as of ancient Italy are the paradoxes we are accustomed to find in any highly civilized, highly complicated, highly endowed human personality in times of trial and temptation, stress and conflict.

We are the remote heirs of Italy's great cultural past, and we have never ceased to draw upon its strengths. Italians, however, are the direct heirs. They live close to that past and can draw upon its strengths as a child draws upon its mother's breast. By the same token, they are close to their own historical weaknesses. And they feel free—in whatever sense man is free within the limitations of circumstance and environment—to choose between their ancient strengths and weaknesses. No nation of men believes more passionately than Italians in man's freedom of will. None understands better that "character is destiny," and that a choice always exists between right and wrong, good and evil. The "miracle of Italy" in the last decade is simply this: Italians chose, despite defeat and poverty, to build a better Italy. They chose *not* to despair.

As is true with all nations, the strengths and weaknesses of modern Italy reside in the character of its citizens. If one who has worked and lived in Italy may be permitted a wide generalization, the great strength of the Italian character lies in the capacity for courage, patience and resourcefulness. Its weaknesses lie in a surfeit of the historical spirit, which is prone to be one of scepticism and sometimes cynical improvisation.

Nevertheless, in viewing the Italian picture today, especially the political picture, it is we who must show patience. We must remember that for generations Italians have had no long or deep-rooted *tradition* of government to sustain them, guide them and form them, and that

the present generation is no exception. For most of its 100 "modern" years, Italy was a monarchy, which, though it began as a parliamentary democracy, lapsed into an authoritarian dictatorship before it was finally destroyed in 1946. Its "tradition" of moderate republican rule has barely reached the age of consent, much less of consensus. The Republic of Italy, founded only 15 years ago, is just barely a teen-age democracy. That such gigantic economic and cultural progress has been made under the 15-year-old Republic—torn by political dissension and factionalism—once again gives us the clue: the Italian people themselves have made it, because they have *willed* economic progress, even though they have not yet willed political harmony.

Mr. Kubly is not an economist, sociologist or historian. He is a man of letters. But he has lived closely and compassionately among the Italian people. He has understood this great fact: that the Italian people themselves are making (even improvising) a new Italy, in spite of every material and political obstacle. His account, while of necessity impressionistic and artistic (that is, subjective), is nevertheless rich, vivid and warm. His introduction to the most paradoxical, fascinating and often inspiring young republic of the West can be profitably read by everyone who has ever known or dreamed of knowing Italy.

CLARE BOOTHE LUCE
former U.S. Ambassador to Italy

1

The Country of the Human Heart

THE gate to Italy is Naples. Here you are in a world of the senses, for Italy is a land of sensuousness—and sights, sounds and smells are most vigorous in Naples.

A matron leaning from a third-floor window is unfurling her wash like ship's pennants across the Via San Biagio de' Librari and doing a passable job of singing *Sempre libera* from Giuseppe Verdi's opera *La Traviata*. A *pasta* peddler circles with his cart to avoid the drip of the wash. At a street-corner shrine a widow wearing her grief like a cloak kneels silently, her great eyes yet taking in the vigorous life about her. A donkey brays. You smell fish and the sea, roasting chestnuts, wisteria and festering garbage.

Down by the bay, one of the most beautiful in the world, boys' naked bodies are flashing in the sea, and a long file of straining fishermen and their wives are pulling in a net. One of the newer legends in Naples is of a mermaid netted during the wartime occupation and served roasted to a visiting American general.

Not far from the bay, at the spiritual center of the city, is the 19th Century Galleria, a glass

9

labyrinth ringing with amplified popular music and swarming with nuns, beggars, streetwalkers, peddlers and lovers. Under one roof you can buy a Borsalino hat, a Martini cocktail, a boat ticket to Capri, a sacred statue—and many another product and service desired by man.

Across Via Vittorio Emmanuele III is the elegant San Carlo opera house. Under the canopy in front, a political speaker is shouting to bystanders for the return of the monarchy, and through an open door a noted soprano can be heard rehearsing *La Gioconda*.

YOU will know by now that you are in the land of human nature. Emotions and sensations are fulfilled and externalized, and everything is communicated. It is locally rumored that the only psychiatrists in Italy are those serving the foreign diplomatic and commercial colonies. The Italian fulfills each of life's moments, without an Anglo-Saxon's waste on regret for the past or hope for the future. His only frustration is poverty, and he can make a scherzo even of that, as do the street boys merrily laughing their singsong, "*Ho fame*, I am hungry."

A humpback in white approaches in a cloud of white dust. He could almost be Pulcinella, traditional Neapolitan clown, parent of England's Punch. Actually, he is a baker carrying flour sacks, but it's all the same. Naples, built like an amphitheater on its famous bay, is an eternally unfolding play by the best actors in the world. The comedy is broad and the tragedy cruel, and the curtain never rings down.

Americans arriving at Italy's third largest city feel at once a warm familiarity. For Neapolitans are emigrators, and the "Little Italys" of America's cities are populated with these slight, dark, dynamic and articulate people. The bustle of Naples is the same as on Manhattan's Mulberry Street or San Francisco's North Beach.

Italy, however, is not one land but many, and the human landscape is as variable as the geographic. There are no "typical Italians"—not the Neapolitans, anyway. Other emigrators are the Sicilians, more silent than Scotsmen and prouder than the Irish. The seafaring Genoese,

taller, black-haired and boastful, are known to the world as waiters, stewards and sailors on ships. Less traveled are the stout brown-haired Tuscans, their wide brows like those shown in Etruscan paintings; the suave white-skinned Venetians, who seem more like Spaniards; the Lombards, some of whom are fair as their Germanic ancestors; and the diminutive Sards of Sardinia, among the dourest people on earth.

Bounded on three sides by the sea and on the north by the Alps, Italy is, practically speaking, an island. It is divided as if by a cross, the Apennines cleaving it almost all the way from top to bottom like the spiny dorsal fin of a fish, and the great Po River cutting across its North from Piedmont's glaciers to the green Adriatic Sea. The northwest is highly industrial, the northeast agricultural; and except for the fertile Apulian plain in the southeast, the South is largely an arid stony wretchedness with hardly any difference between the two sides of the mountains.

The northwest, booming with commerce, is another Italy in which an American may feel at home. Its center is Milan, the country's second largest population center, called by other Italians "the American city." Milan has supermarkets, corner gas stations, installment buying and a rising skyline of steel and glass office buildings, banks and apartments. As a Milanese once said, "Rome has politics, ruins and the Pope, but Milan is the real capital—financial, commercial, industrial, musical, artistic, theatrical, publishing, jazz and stripteasing. What more do you want?"

BECAUSE of the feverish pace of a man from Milan, a Roman refers to anyone who can't relax, no matter where he comes from, as a "Milanese." The Milanese attributes his own hyperthyroid behavior to an unpleasantly invigorating winter climate, which is comparable in rain, hail, snow, sleet and fog to that of London. "In Rome," said a Milanese, "all you feel like doing is looking out the window."

Italy's weather, indeed, is as varied as its landscape, embracing in an area only about three fourths the size of California all the climates from Sweden to Africa. More snow has been known to fall in the northern valleys than in Iceland, and no visitor lolling in the sun at a seaside winter resort could imagine the tomblike chill of a Tuscan hill town on a wet day in December. Yet the Italian takes his weather in stride—it remains part of his eternal stoicism.

In Italy's northeast are the vast agricultural plains of Emilia-Romagna. Here, on broad-acred commercial farms, American tractors plow the Po's deposits of fertile silt, and oxen pull rubber-tired carts loaded with sugar beets to refineries. Black-robed women sit in circles on barn floors husking corn or combing the long white locks of hemp. The landscape is flat as Illinois, and in the autumn the red brick barns, the corn shocks and turkey flocks and the trees hanging with ripening apples are like an American Thanksgiving scene.

But the cross on the map is not inappropriate, for Italy today is a crucified land in which the fertile plains are an ironic token from an ancient past.

MORE than 2,000 years ago the Apennines were covered by forests. But throughout history Italians when in trouble have felt an urge to chop down their trees. Rome's emperors and later the popes had the trees cut to build ships for their warring navies. Furthermore, wood has always been a staple fuel. With no trees to hold the earth, torrents have washed the topsoil from the crests and hillsides and deposited it in the valleys and the sea, turning the emperors' old lagoon city of Ravenna into an inland town. Floods ravaged the valleys, spreading disease. To salvage the plains, a succession of hydraulic experts, among them the great 15th Century artist and engineer Leonardo da Vinci, designed a system of irrigation still used in Lombardy. The denuded highlands became arid and stony as Greece, frequently too sparse to support life.

Forming a link between North and South are Umbria, Tuscany and northern Latium, regions on whose mountain slopes an intensive pattern of garden farming is maintained. Here olives, grapes, peaches, grain, beans and flowers are grown on a single patch of land the size of an American kitchen garden, and the peasant can maintain his family in comfortable adequacy.

Below the Tuscan-Umbrian bridge there is increasing poverty, right down to the oriental misery of Sicily, 85 miles from Africa. On these lower shores of humanity a donkey is more expensive to maintain than a human being. Much of the South is a vast rural slum of third-class citizens caught in the squalor, violence and vendettas of their archaic earth.

ALMOST everywhere there is stone in the landscape. In Lucania in the South and on the islands of Sicily and Sardinia there are areas in which the gray, wind-polished rock is like a garden of modern sculpture, relieved only by a few stunted pines. From such a homely natural resource springs the Italian genius for building.

Italians are compulsive builders. Their towns are ponderous masses of stone and marble, skillfully cut and fashioned. To the Latin it is a degradation to live in a wooden house. When the poet Torquato Tasso visited Paris in the 16th Century he was shocked by what he considered the barbarous houses of wood, clearly fit only for uncivilized people. Italian house decorations are likely to be stone statues, reliefs and monuments, and any languishing bits of greenery are caged in stone enclosures.

Much of Italy's building has been religious. But the abundance of the country's Romanesque and Gothic cathedrals is the result not of a religious but of an architectural and civic enthusiasm. Only cheap peasant labor combined with a spirit of community sacrifice could make possible so many great churches. An 11th Century chronicle tells how the entire citizenry of Modena, notables and plebeians alike, participated in the planning of a cathedral, and the oldest known vernacular inscription in Rome (1084) is on a mural showing slaves hauling a column. "Your dragging of stones is well deserved," it says, "Pull, you villains!"

Rome! It is the Holy City to which all roads lead. Any road at all will be a shock, for the

Eternal City is girdled by a circle of new apartment buildings, garish pastel-colored constructions rising from the raw earth like low-income American public housing. Rome is in one of its greatest building booms—and one of its most unattractive. You finally enter the ancient city, passing the line of the 2,500-year-old wall at the gate of San Giovanni, and at once you are in a sort of religious world's fair. Nuns and priests seem to float on winds which billow their robes like sails. And what bright sails! No pirate flag was ever more dramatically hoisted than the scarlet cassocks of German seminarians, the blues from Greece and the purples from Scotland. Against them the browns and blacks of America and Ireland are funereal and somber. One wonders if the clergy has heard the old Roman saying, "Faith is made here and believed elsewhere."

SUCH cynicism is characteristic of Italy's most un-Italian city. This seat of religion and government is an island to which people have come and from which they will depart. Its famous hills (there are more than seven and few people can say just which are *the* seven) make a rising and falling sea of churches (some four hundred), campaniles, fountains, statues, palaces, colonnades, forums and gardens.

Today the city of the emperors, refurbished by the architects Michelangelo and Bramante in the 16th Century, decorated by Bernini in the 17th and now augmented by the broad vaulted domes of the contemporary engineer-architect Pier Luigi Nervi, is increasingly a gaudy pleasure carnival for the international rich and carefree, who have discovered its winter climate to be more agreeable than that of Paris. The old streets with their luxurious hotels and expensive shops and restaurants are lit up like aquariums, and some of the ancient grottoes have become neon-illuminated night clubs.

Young Roman aristocrats, Midas-rich, boasting of cardinals, popes and sometimes saints in their family trees, used to occupy themselves with hereditary duties at the Vatican; now all too many pass their self-indulgent lives with high-speed sports cars, American jazz, narcotics and orgiastic parties. To them the Italy outside Rome is a seat for country villas and a source of cheap domestic labor. If there are any true Romans in the city, they are the *Trasteverini*, the quarrelsome, fun-loving laboring clans that live in the quarter of Trastevere "beyond the Tiber."

High- or low-born, an Italian hates solitude. He loves the crowd and is happiest in the market place and the street. His passion for public gatherings and for life in the open air is as old as his civilization. The piazza, descendant of the Roman forum and the center of every village, was created expressly to satisfy the Italian's passion for communal life. Ever since the Caesars, Italians have been masters of oratory. In the middle of the 12th Century the German bishop Otto von Freising complained of "long-winded sermons after the Italian fashion." As the political speech began to replace the sermon in public persuasion, "orator" became the designation for an Italian ambassador. In a country where the lower classes are still semi-literate, public speaking remains the instrument of popular education and eloquence is a national trait.

GREGARIOUSNESS, curiosity and a fondness for communicating make Italians a universal people, the most universal in Europe. The provincial peasant with whom you share a railroad compartment is completely at home in your company. He may be part of a delegation traveling to a papal audience and it may be his first trip to Rome, but he is nonetheless a citizen of the world. At noontime he will offer you a chunk of his bread with slices of salami and a handful of shiny black olives. He will hand you his Chianti bottle with the crumbs from his lips still clinging to it. You are his traveling companion, and so he will want to know all about you. How much did your suit cost and where was the fabric woven? How long did it take you to cross the ocean? Have you ever been in Bridgeport, where he has relatives?

The peasant's love affair with the universe is his heritage from the peripatetic Romans who conquered the ancient world. The Caesars made themselves living symbols of universalism. Vergil and Livy gave form to the dream of a world community in their writings. A long history of invasions and occupations added to the original Roman and Etruscan blood the restless genes of Greeks and Goths, Normans, Spaniards and Moors. Through such a mixed strain, cosmopolitanism flows naturally. Pope Gregory the Great built a world-wide Christian community to which Thomas Aquinas gave the intellectual substance and Dante, humanistic poetry. Marco Polo's yearning for exotic civilizations turned him eastward, and the curiosity of Christopher Columbus and Amerigo Vespucci sent them west. Galileo explored the heavens.

Under imperial Rome and later under the popes Italy was a collection of cities, each its own nation and its own world. The Italian has no "fatherland" in the German sense. His energies and talents have always been too vast to be limited by geographic boundaries. An Italian's "native land"—the only one that has always been free of foreign domination—is his art and learning, the universal world of Dante, of Leonardo and Michelangelo, of Galileo and Enrico Fermi, of Giuseppe Verdi.

How does one cope with a country that is really a constellation of many little countries; how does one choose the representative? A hill town in Umbria, perhaps—one not overrun with tourists.

NORTH of Rome, perched on a huge platform of tufa rock 600 feet high, is Orvieto, which gave its name to a wonderful wine and has a beautiful cathedral known as "the golden lily." Arrive at sunset from the south and you will see a great oval island, its spires rising from a rose-tinted cloud, as radiant as a vision from the Apocalypse.

If it is grape season, the gutters will be purple with leavings, as if wine were flowing in the streets. The Gothic cathedral is on the edge of a precipice and you will come upon it suddenly. Its façade presents a lacy pattern of saints, apostles and prophets grouped in golden mosaic about the Virgin.

Go into a restaurant near the cathedral. Most probably the restaurateur is also a wine maker and will take you into his cellars. The soft rock under the town has been hollowed into wine caves. The restaurateur—let's call him Attilio— has many large barrels, and with a glass pipette he asks you to sample them all—white wines dry and delicate as distilled sunlight, red wines that are heavier and sweeter. In the new wine there are many flies, but these, Attilio assures you, are harmless, being dead. A velvety mold covers barrels and walls like snow, and on the ceilings are stalactites of mold.

WITH a flashlight you move up and down stairs carved from rock. Orvieto is a ceramic center, and in one of the caves Attilio has a potter's wheel, powered by a treadle. With lightning speed he turns a beautiful shape. Secretly in the semidarkness he will show you a finished vase, glazed with slightly bawdy scenes in an Etruscan spirit. At this moment you are probably under the cathedral itself, and Attilio tells you that farther down the hillside, dug into the side of the precipice, are Etruscan tombs.

You return to the surface just as the evening prayer bells begin to ring out. A donkey carrying baskets of grapes passes in the darkness and the owner, carrying a cask on his head, makes the sign of the cross.

Italy? Orvieto is neither Naples' Italy nor Milan's. It is a less known and gentler Italy and perhaps a truer one, for in its blend of Christianity and classical paganism it is more than any other city the humanist Italy of tradition.

Rural Italy is more Greek than Roman, for the Romans of the Empire were urban people, and Italy is still largely an agricultural land of shepherds and soil tillers. Since before history man and nature have collaborated to mold the earth to unchanging patterns. Sheep graze on the turf floors of Greek temples in Segesta and Paestum. The young peasant shepherding them and the bride who waits for him under the olives might be Daphnis and Chloë.

A foreigner on his first visit to Italy feels a familiarity with the landscape about him because he recognizes the image that famous artists and poets have created. During the great centuries of religious art, Italy was the most painted country in the world, and the landscapes we have thought of as Biblical since our childhood are really Italian. Christ entering Jerusalem? He is really a young Tuscan vintner riding a donkey into the towered town of San Gimignano. The Nativity star? It shines over goatskin-clad shepherds in the Florentine hills. The flight into Egypt? It is the artist's family riding over the moonlit Umbrian mountains.

Biblical animals—the ponderous ox and the capricious donkey—share the peasant's labor. The horse, considered an aristocratic animal, is never used for tilling the soil.

BUT the Italy of the ancient pastures is changing, more transformed by World War II and its aftermath than any other country in Europe. Tourism, a feature of Italy for three hundred years, has become a leading industry, the number of visitors exceeding 16 million a year. While the influx has brought revenue and the pleasures of social exchange, it has also brought discontent, for the Italian is too proud to fit easily into the role of servant in his own house. Any middle-class American on a first visit seems to him like a self-indulgent millionaire. His discontent is stirred, too, by American motion pictures, which are his cheapest and favorite entertainment. Not fond of Italian neorealistic films, which are too representative of his own life, he believes that the luxury and crime fantasies of Hollywood are equally representative of American life.

Most Italians are warmly pro-American. What anti-Americanism exists was analyzed poignantly by a young Florentine clerk named Tullio when he said, "With Americans we Italians are very much like a cast-off lover. We say Americans who can have everything they want care only for what they can possess. We say they have no spirit and no love and we are contemptuous of Americans who have no soul, for we are Italians who live in the soul. We say we do not care about the things that Americans care

about. But that is not true. We care for them too, only we fear we can never have them. So we pretend that we do not want them. We pretend to hate Americans. But we do not hate them. To us they are really gods whom we worship and love. It is very hard for us to be honest for, you see, we are also very proud."

In the past 15 years friendly countries have come to Italy with gifts and loans and with medical and technical assistance, and the results are apparent. They are manifested by teeming, prosperous Milan, the American hay-balers on the plains of the Po, the end of malaria both on the mainland and on the islands, the drained marshes turned into productive farms in Sardinia. There are also billboards on the Appian Way, and the ancient road to Ostia is a tunnel of advertisements for everything from cooking gas to American soft drinks. The war between the old and the new is everywhere in evidence.

In a Tuscan church not long ago a corner of a fresco by the Florentine artist Benozzo Gozzoli was scraped away to make room for an electric-light switch. Tullio was horrified. "To destroy a masterpiece to make a switch for electricity —that is disgraceful," he said. Then he added thoughtfully, "We are becoming more American than we think. It has become more important to have switches for electricity than to have paintings."

NOT surprisingly, Italy becomes less anti-American as it becomes more Americanized. The changes have not solved its problems, however. Never the idyllic Arcadia that dreamers and poets have imagined, it has been an unhappy, if beautiful, land. Its tragedy is the disenchantment of experience, of history as a heap of ruins. Yet Pulcinella's smiling face still greets the world, and the optimism, the ebullience, the everlasting joy in being alive which is the real genius of Italy has never diminished. In return for its living gift of art—music, painting, architecture, sculpture, literature — humanity owes Italy a debt not redeemable with a few loans and aid plans. The western world, after all, owes its soul to Italy.

Youthful Romans frolic by the splashing waters of the Trevi fountain. A coin cast into the pool is said to ensure a visitor's return

The Verve of a Timeless Folk

Irrepressible energy and indomitable physical hardihood, common to both young and old, endow Italian life with an ebullience that wells forth like the ever-present fountains. Children bright with smiles dance in city streets from morning until late in the night, village housewives are forever achatter, and fathers and husbands top the day's work with a wine-tinted song. Only when the pace slackens and the noise abates do Italy's other moods come to the fore.

SIMPLICITY AND SPLENDOR, *in unending counterpoint, vie to dominate life and landscape, as countless villages cleave to ways they followed when Venice's glory was still young*

HEART OF A VILLAGE, the spring-fed fountain in the hill town of Desulo in Sardinia has always been the place where women get together to wash clothes and to gossip.

CROWN OF A CITY, the Piazza San Marco in Venice (*opposite*), shown flooded by a high tide, mirrors the cathedral and *campanile* that Venetians count among their gems.

In Florence's noble Piazza della Signoria, the dawn light caresses a replica of Michelangelo's David, framed by the torso and legs of

a Roman lion. Across the square, near a row of Renaissance mansions, Ammannati's Neptune commands a fountain of Tritons and naiads

GAY HUES *add*
a brightness to the
daily life of Italians,
whether they are
trading, chatting with
friends or just lolling

BUSTLING GALLERIA in the heart
of Naples is lit by the sun's glare,
which streams through arched sky-
lights. Shops of all kinds line the
elaborate central terrazzo walkway,
with its clusters of shaded tables.

CROWDED BEACH at Rimini, on
the northern Adriatic, sparkles all
summer long with multi-colored
windbreaks and low-slung canvas
chairs. The close-knit Italian family invariably takes the baby along.

ENTICING DISPLAY of ripe watermelons exemplifies the pride with which even the humblest of Italian retailers advertises his wares and his artistic abilities. Setting up shop early, peddlers spend hours culling and arranging the goods they offer for sale.

A MUTED BEAUTY surrounds the dead: As fog shrouds the cedars on Venice's cemetery isle of San Michele, a woman adorns the grave of a beloved one. This unusual scene was photographed by Ernst Haas.

An Imperial Legacy

CONSIDERING the human addiction to wishful thinking and uninhibited hindsight, it is not surprising that the recorded history of any people often tends to be a romantic blend of myth and reality. This is particularly so in the case of such a venerable and complex country as Italy.

The job of separating fact from fancy over two and a half millenniums may be made easier, however, if Italy's story—up until the country's emergence into the modern era a century and a half ago—is divided into four periods. The first covers the founding of the Roman Republic and its expansion into an empire. The second is the age of the Caesars and the Empire's decline. The third takes Italy through the chaotic centuries of the Middle Ages, while the fourth is that of the Renaissance and its aftermath. In each of these four periods there are legends aplenty, but it is generally possible to weigh them in the proper perspective of their time.

Ecco the libretto! The earliest of Italy's myths holds that Rome was founded some 27 centuries ago on the Palatine Hill by Romulus, who was sired by Mars and suckled by a wolf. In a fit of rivalry, like Cain in the Bible, he killed his twin brother Remus. To provide his followers with wives he arranged the celebrated conquest of the Sabine women.

In reality, however, Italian history starts with tribes like the Villanovans, Sabines and Ligurians, who lived on the peninsula from the earliest days of history. The name "Italy" comes from a word used by one of the tribes meaning "calf-land." The most advanced of the early peoples were the Etruscans, seafarers who moved into north-central Italy, probably from Asia Minor, around 800 B.C. Competent in war, the Etruscans conquered the native kingdom on the Roman hills and set up their own monarchs.

The Romans overthrew their Etruscan kings in 509 B.C., establishing a republic which was governed by two elected consuls, an advisory Senate and a popular Assembly. But the Republic was at first dominated by wealthy landowners, who protected themselves against the poor by denying them a voice in politics. Even then the people were forming themselves into two groups—the haves and have-nots, or patricians and plebeians—as they have done more or less consistently in Italy ever since.

HAVING inherited the Etruscans' lust for conquest, the Romans undertook expansions of their own. They formed alliances with friendly tribes, subdued others, and spent the next two and a half centuries conquering the entire peninsula south of the Arno River. As a reward for fighting, the plebeians were given limited representation in the government.

Being masters on land, the Romans turned to the sea. Jealous of the might of Carthage, a marauding North African sea power centered in the area of present-day Tunisia, they attacked. During the century-long Punic Wars (the name comes from the Greco-Latin word for the Phoenicians, who had founded Carthage), Sicily,

Sardinia and Corsica, as well as northern Italy, were annexed to Rome. The great Carthaginian general, Hannibal, marched with his elephants through Spain and southern France and over the Alps to attack the Romans on the peninsula, but he was ultimately defeated in 202 B.C. by a young Roman general named Scipio Africanus, who had in the meantime conquered Spain. Finally, in 146 B.C., Carthage itself became a Roman province. Rome was now the dominant power in the western Mediterranean.

DURING this period, Rome's ruling classes had developed a liking for the more hedonistic arts and philosophies of Greece. When Macedonia and Syria threatened to destroy the independence of the Greek cities, the Romans attacked and defeated the transgressors, thereby making the Greeks dependent on Rome. It is from this period of acquisition of Hellenistic art and legend that the world has its image of the Romans as noble and enlightened warriors, guided by their destiny to rule the world.

Actually Rome's ruling patricians were not extraordinary fighters—they usually got others to do the battling for them. But they were superb both as efficient administrators and as grand larcenists. Newly conquered areas were economically exploited. With riches flowing in from the colonies, Rome developed quickly into a nation of plutocrats.

Shiploads of slaves were brought from the east to work large estates. The slaves displaced free workers, who then poured into the cities and swelled the ranks of urban plebeians. In the craze for foreign pleasure and novelties, moral corruption permeated all the classes. No one listened when the elderly Cato pleaded for a return to the stoic virtues of early Rome—simplicity of life, honesty and family loyalty.

The land-poor Roman plebeians were the first to revolt, but their rebellion spread to other peoples on the Italian peninsula. During a decade of civil and social warring, more than half a million persons died.

The slaves revolted next. A Thracian slave named Spartacus led a rebellion of 120,000 men in 73 B.C., and for three years stood off the best soldiers Rome could send against him. When Spartacus was finally defeated by the numerical superiority of the Romans, 6,000 of his followers were nailed to crosses on the Appian Way, the famous road leading south from Rome.

Clearly the situation was getting out of hand. Rome had become a parasitical state and its republican government was unfit to administer an empire. To ward off disaster a strong man was needed. Waiting in the wings was Julius Caesar.

Born in 100 B.C.—direct descent from Jupiter was *his* myth—he had shown himself a winning general in a series of wars culminating in the conquest of Gaul. On his way back home in 49 B.C. he was ordered by the Senate and by his rival Pompey, Rome's ruler, to disband his army before entering Italy. Instead, crying out "The die is cast!" he ceremoniously crossed a border stream near Rimini called the Rubicon, and as Italy's first *duce* made his march on Rome. Pompey fled, and Caesar became chief of state.

Caesar went on to quell revolts in Asia Minor, from which he filed one of the tersest military dispatches in history: "I came, I saw, I conquered." He returned with many ideas for social reform—and did carry out some of these. But his efforts were cut short. In 44 B.C., shortly after being elected dictator for life, Caesar was stabbed to death by Brutus, a patrician senator.

BRUTUS' dagger introduced Italy's second great period of history, because it brought into power Caesar's heir and grandnephew, Octavian, and inaugurated two centuries of astonishing peace and prosperity. In his 42-year rule Octavian built 82 temples and many libraries, theaters and roads, and tried (with little success) to reform Roman morals. A grateful Senate gave Octavian the title of Augustus, "the increasing god," and he became, in effect, the first Roman emperor. By this time religion and patriotism were becoming inseparable in Rome, and emperor worship would soon be every citizen's duty.

During the reign of Octavian's successor Tiberius, there was a minor disturbance and an execution in a distant and insignificant province. It went unnoticed in Rome. The name of the crucified man was Jesus.

An emperor's method of ensuring approved succession was to adopt a favorite, usually a relative, as his son. This has resulted in a remarkably tangled imperial genealogy. Octavian was thus Julius Caesar's adopted son, but he was also his grandnephew. Tiberius was a stepson of Octavian, and was succeeded by his great-nephew Caligula, a madman who was also Octavian's great-grandson. Caligula was succeeded—after his assassination by the Praetorian Guard—by his uncle Claudius, who was also Tiberius' nephew. The last of the nepotistically tangled Julio-Claudian emperors (those who were related to Julius Caesar) was Nero, who committed suicide at 32. In the 18 months after Nero, three emperors met violent deaths. And so it went, decade after decade, through the Twelve Caesars catalogued for history by the Roman biographer Suetonius.

Beginning in 98 A.D., Rome was ruled by the enormously gifted Spanish-born emperor, Trajan, who conquered Romania, Armenia and Mesopotamia and built the Trajan Forum. Trajan was succeeded by his nephew (and adopted son) Hadrian, the most brilliant of all the emperors. Hadrian was all things—intellectual, poet, astrologer, traveler, swashbuckler and, above everything, humanistic champion of the common man. He constructed a magnificent tomb for himself on the river Tiber, which in the Middle Ages took on the name of Castel Sant' Angelo. Outside Rome at Tivoli he built the noblest villa of antiquity.

ALMOST as remarkable as Hadrian was the Stoic Marcus Aurelius, who ruled from 161 to 180. He quelled uprisings in central Europe and wrote his *Meditations*, a classic of Roman literature. At his death in 180, however, the Roman Empire was past its peak and had begun to decline. It was a huge complex of prosperous cities, most of them self-governing, and all of them with magnificent buildings. Rome had adopted and absorbed Hellenistic culture and had spread it through the entire civilized West.

Rome's way of life was both wonderful and horrible, with immeasurable significance to later ages. Europeans and Americans are all its heirs —and so are modern Russians, whose ancestors were part of the Eastern Roman Empire. In addition to the manifest legacy of architecture, Rome enriched civilization with perfected styles of poetry and prose and with a use of rhetorical argument that has never been surpassed. By far Rome's greatest gifts, however, were governmental: an effective system of political administration and a body of law based largely on jurisprudence rather than legislation.

But the capital of civilization also had large defects, and these spelled its doom. The upper classes were too prosperous and apathetic, the lower classes too oppressed and discontented. Largely absent was the great binding force of any democratic society, a middle class. Governments, even with benevolent rulers, were autocratic. The Romans, softened by luxury, seemed suddenly to have lost their nerve.

So in the Third Century began a turbulent descent. In less than 100 years Rome had 33 emperors, almost all of whom died violently. One of them, Decius, began the slaughter of Christians who had refused to worship the emperors. The Christians were dissenters who, while performing their rites secretly in underground catacombs, were organizing a strong, coherent organization throughout Rome's dominions. This new organization, placing its loyalty in an authority higher than worldly empire, was considered a threat to the Roman state. When bad times came, the Christians were natural scapegoats.

IN an effort to strengthen governmental administration in the crumbling Empire, the Emperor Diocletian divided the vast domain into East and West. Diocletian was the last of the great emperors to persecute Christians, and with Constantine the Roman carnival was over.

Constantine began as the weakest of four competitive rulers. *His* myth is that during the Battle of Milvian Bridge he saw a cross in the heavens bearing the words, "By this sign thou shalt conquer." Ordering his soldiers to mark their shields with the symbol of Christ, he went on to defeat the enemy. The year was 312. The Christians emerged from their underground and churches rose throughout the Empire. Constantine himself built the first basilica of St. Peter's in Rome, after which he moved his capital to the eastern city of Byzantium, renamed for him Constantinople.

By changing the religion of the greatest empire in history, Constantine did more than any other single ruler to mold western civilization. When he died, ancient Rome also died. Christ had triumphed over Caesar, and the Fourth Century, which had begun with pagans persecuting Christians, ended with Christians persecuting pagans. Italy's second great period of history was over.

A long decline now began. For one century (376 to 476) the weakened Western Empire was overrun by invaders—Visigoths, Vandals (who added their name to language) and finally the paint-daubed Huns. The weakened emperors fled to Ravenna. In 476 the last Roman Emperor of the West, Romulus Augustulus, was deposed by invaders, and the Italian peninsula fell under Gothic rule. In principle the Gothic kings were subordinates of the emperor in Constantinople—but in practice they were nothing of the kind.

For centuries Italy was a starving, illiterate, plague-ridden agrarian land, struggling through the heavy night of the so-called Dark Ages. The novelist Elizabeth Bowen has described this interim between the Rome of the Caesars and the Rome of the Renaissance—Italy's third historical period—as being "like a long, bad, overpacked, overwritten historical novel."

Some important events and personalities light up the darkness like flares. In the beginning of the period the Roman Empire in the East took on a Byzantine character, becoming generally Greek in culture and coming under the control of people of eastern origin. The most famous of the emperors in the East, Justinian, tried to

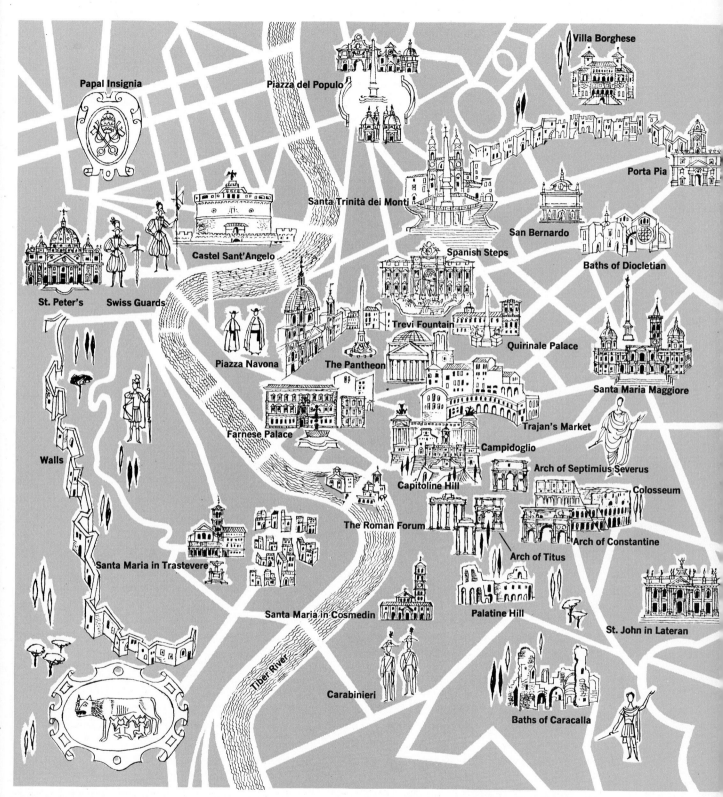

Papal Insignia

Piazza del Populo

Villa Borghese

Santa Trinità dei Monti

Porta Pia

Castel Sant'Angelo

San Bernardo

Spanish Steps

Baths of Diocletian

St. Peter's

Swiss Guards

Trevi Fountain

Quirinale Palace

Piazza Navona

The Pantheon

Santa Maria Maggiore

Farnese Palace

Trajan's Market

Campidoglio

Walls

Capitoline Hill

Arch of Septimius Severus

Colosseum

The Roman Forum

Arch of Constantine

Arch of Titus

Santa Maria in Trastevere

Santa Maria in Cosmedin

Palatine Hill

St. John in Lateran

Tiber River

Carabinieri

Baths of Caracalla

THE ROME OF HISTORY as it appears today is shown in an artist's conception. At the lower left are Romulus, the city's mythical founder, and his brother Remus. Above them and at top right are sections from the old wall, with later buildings attached. Descendants of the early Romans live in the Trastevere section to the left of the Tiber.

29

return the West to active imperial rule. But he failed, and is remembered for the ornate, mosaic-filled churches which he and his wife Theodora built in their western capital of Ravenna, and for codifying the old Roman law, thereby purifying it and making it intact for study through the ages.

Though in theory Rome was being ruled from Constantinople, the popes, who headed the Christian Church at Rome, looked upon themselves as the true heirs to the Caesars' Western Empire. The emperor in the East, they reasoned, was only a man, and far removed from the day-to-day needs of Rome. Popes, as supreme pontiffs representing God on earth, were masters of men. Hence, emperors were to obey the popes' will, which was interpreted as being God's will also. The Eastern emperors refused to be coerced; and thus was struck the battle between church and state that was to plague Italy for centuries.

The popes finally decided to ignore the Constantinople rulers and create another emperor. In the Sixth Century the great Christian administrator, Pope Gregory the Great, took on the role if not the title of emperor in the West and declared himself spiritual ruler over all Christendom. The way was paved, and on Christmas Day in the year 800 the mighty Frankish king, Charlemagne, wearing the white chlamys (short mantle) and sandals of a Roman patrician, was crowned emperor in St. Peter's by Pope Leo III. The act was a proclamation to the world that the Roman Empire in the West was not dead—and that the popes created the emperors.

BUT the entry upon the Italian scene of the greatest ruler of the Middle Ages did not produce the miracle for which the Romans had hoped. Charlemagne, a foreigner, was never popular in Italy, and by crowning him in Rome the Pope had merely succeeded in conceiving one of the most preposterous myths of history: the political anachronism later entitled the Holy Roman Empire. It had little sustained reality as a political unit, and Voltaire later remarked that it was neither holy, nor Roman, nor an empire. The new emperors were to turn against the papacy and almost succeeded in wrecking it. For four snarled centuries good popes, bad popes and antipopes struggled for influence and survival with emperors, European monarchs and rebellious noble families.

Outside of Rome, life on the Italian peninsula was primarily rural, with land ownership the hereditary right of princelings who had been rewarded for personal services to popes and emperors. Such a system left a majority of the people servile peasants, little better than slaves.

IN the 12th Century a strong emperor, Frederick Barbarossa, came down from Germany to claim his right to be crowned Holy Roman Emperor. Frederick happened to be related to both of Germany's two great warring feudal families, the Welfs and the Hohenstaufens. He was opposed in Italy by an alliance consisting of the papacy and a "Lombard League" of cities, which he fought under the banner of the Hohenstaufens, known to Italians as Ghibellines (from their pronunciation of Waiblingen, the German name of a Hohenstaufen village). The anti-Ghibelline alliance became known as the Guelphs (from Welf), and the conflict was the beginning of a number of Guelph-Ghibelline wars between coalitions of states led by popes and coalitions led by emperors, wars which were to darken Italy until well into the Renaissance. Frederick was defeated, but his son Henry VI, taking up the cudgels, won the Sicilian kingdom, which included the southern part of the peninsula.

Henry's freethinking son, Frederick II (1194-1250), was the most gifted of the Holy Roman Emperors, a Renaissance man who predated the Renaissance by nearly two centuries. To his lavish castles in Apulia and Sicily he brought scholars, astrologers, troubadours and lawyers, many of them eastern Jews and Mohammedans. His court was the intellectual center of the West. Frederick also founded the University of Naples, where he trained professional jurists to bring about his greatest reform, the withholding of criminal jurisdiction from feudal nobles.

Frederick left the regency of Apulia and Sicily to the favorite of his six sons, the illegitimate Manfred, Prince of Taranto. Possessing his father's enlightenment but with a blither spirit, Manfred reigned over his court at Palermo as the King of Troubadours, dressed always in green, the color of hope. Championing the Ghibellines against the popes, he sent raids into the northern provinces. After his defeat in 1266, France took over the South. A few years later Sicily came under the control of Spain.

Meanwhile the Guelph-Ghibelline wars raged more savagely than ever. In Rome the powerful noble families of Colonna (Ghibelline) and Orsini (Guelph) turned old ruins into private family fortresses and battled each other. The chaos finally culminated in the self-exile of the popes from Rome to the French town of Avignon (1309–1378). This "Babylonian captivity" gave France an imposing papal court and turned the popes into sycophants of the French kings.

But Italy's long night seemed at last to be ending. The continued factional feuding in Tuscany, Lombardy, Emilia and Romagna put the independent cities into the hands of strong families—the Visconti of Milan, the Este of Ferrara, the Malatesta of Rimini, the Gonzaga of Mantua. Leaderless Siena sank into an exhausted decline, but Florence, under the powerful and resourceful Medici family, launched a great artistic movement which rose over the civilized world like a dazzling rocket. It began Italy's fourth historical period and is famed today as the Italian Renaissance.

AN intellectual bridge for Italy—and finally for all western Europe—from the Dark Ages to early modern times, the Renaissance is difficult to circumscribe with dates. Frederick II had certainly foreshadowed it. During the 14th Century, Italian merchants and bankers were founding great fortunes, and their capital increased commerce, thereby quickening the transfer of ideas within Italy. At the same time three Tuscan writers, Dante, Petrarch and Boccaccio, by creating a distinctively Italian literary style, were establishing the Tuscan dialect (one of the many differing corruptions of ancient Latin) as the language of culture and manners for the whole country. In 1439 Cosimo de' Medici, the first of his family to use his riches for the advancement of art and letters, lured a group of eastern scholars and churchmen to Florence and organized a Platonic Academy. The "new learning," which Florence seized upon, freed men's minds from exclusive domination by Roman Church dogma and exposed them to Greek philosophy and humanism.

The resulting cultural boom permeated all urban society. "Renaissance men" were highly intellectual and cultured business leaders who in their well-rounded lives ran their businesses and towns, patronized artists and writers, sponsored academies, built churches and villas and organized pageants and festivals. The greatest of these was Cosimo de' Medici's grandson, Lorenzo the Magnificent, who, in addition to fulfilling the expected family responsibilities, wrote poetry and became the most eminent art patron of history.

BUT golden ages never last long, and the Renaissance in Italy was no exception. The worldly, luxury-loving popes more and more resembled the pagan emperors of antiquity. Rome, without native writers and artists, was a city of courtiers currying the favors of popes, cardinals, princes and great families. Christian restraint was loosened, with immorality and profligacy the rule.

In 1517 the German priest Martin Luther, shocked by clerical corruption, nailed to the church door in Wittenberg his 95 theses inviting debate on the lucrative Church practice of selling indulgences. Luther was excommunicated, but his challenge resulted in the Protestant Reformation. Two years later the remarkable Hapsburg anti-reformer, Charles V of Spain, became Holy Roman Emperor, and two of the most dynamic men of the 16th Century were pitted against each other in a struggle for the control of man's thought.

Charles was a religious zealot who was determined to stamp out Luther's heresy, and

Luther was equally determined to reform the Roman Church. By a series of religious and dynastic wars Charles kept the Reformation out of most of his dominions and made Milan, Florence, Genoa and the papacy into virtual Hapsburg vassals. The combination of war and the Inquisition, although it saved the Church, broke the spirit of the Renaissance. By the time Charles finally renounced his throne in 1556 to become a religious recluse, Italy had become just a pawn in Europe's power politics.

Only the papacy continued to be a force. Rome's answer to Luther had been a few reforms within the Church itself. In Paris the aristocratic Spanish priest Ignatius of Loyola had founded the Jesuits, a dedicated, highly spiritual group who won the Pope's approval of new reforms. The Italians, having had no strong moral discipline for centuries, reacted to Loyola and other pietists with a wave of relief and joy.

BY the time the so-called Counter Reformation was over at the end of the 16th Century, Italy, like Spain, was once again firmly under the control of the Roman Church. For two centuries thereafter, while Europe's northern countries explored new political, social and economic principles to fit the changing times, Italy remained in a torpor of dogma and orthodoxy.

Ironically, the two Italian inventions of credit banking and double-entry bookkeeping were helping to make possible the great commercial revolutions sweeping Europe, but Italy dozed on. More important, the new capitalism was creating in Europe a great politically stabilizing middle class, while in Italy, as the shadow of feudalism lingered, the arrangement of opposing classes of aristocrats and peasants—like Rome's patricians and plebeians—continued. The country was a battleground for European armies and diplomats, and the flow of taxes was toward Vienna or Madrid. Soon it became fashionable for tourists to travel to Italy to muse over the fates of the Caesars.

One independent neighboring state, the Duchy of Savoy, which included much of present-day Piedmont, was strategically placed to control the important Alpine passes between France and Italy. In the early 18th Century a clever Duke of Savoy, Victor Amadeus II, participated in a war between the major powers of Europe and as a reward was given the island of Sicily. He exchanged Sicily for Sardinia, after which the Savoy holdings, including Piedmont, were known as the Kingdom of Sardinia. It was a development of great significance to the subsequent history of Italy.

DURING most of the 18th Century the popes in Rome, who ruled the Papal States in the center of the peninsula, adopted a position of neutrality between the Austrian Hapsburgs in the North and the Spanish Bourbons in the South. Then along came Napoleon—himself an imperialist—taking the French Revolution outside France. His troops accelerated the spread of the idea of political freedom and hatred for the privileged classes. Against such ideas the papacy, weakened by its own internal troubles, was defenseless. And even in disorganized and backward Italy there were men who had already felt with passion the new spirit from Paris.

As a result Napoleon was welcomed at first by the Italians and eventually took over the whole peninsula. He kidnaped the Pope, sending him to France; he organized all Italy into separate states under his direct or indirect control, and he prodded the Austrian Francis II into abandoning the title of Holy Roman Emperor, thereby ending in ignominy the odd "Empire" so hopefully begun with Charlemagne a thousand years earlier. For the first time in centuries Italy had one master.

Napoleon's downfall in 1815 brought many of the former rulers back, including the Pope. But the seeds wafted from France had taken root. Secret societies turned into political parties. Poets and dramatists celebrated the undying genius of the Italian people. Orators in the piazzas exclaimed that the descendants of Rome alone were qualified to lead the march of civilization into a future of self-conscious nationalism. The modern era was at hand, and the forces of unification began to gather.

Picnicking by the Appian Way, a Roman family proceeds with lunch, ignoring the Second Century Villa of the Quintilii across the road

A Past Eternally Present

Nowhere are specters of the past more palpable than in Italy. A Roman family bent on an *al fresco* lunch will bring along a bottle of Frascati wine, perhaps pressed at the site of Nero's stepfather's villa; they will drive over the Appian Way, built by the Censor Appius Claudius Caecus in 312 B.C., and camp beside a mansion that wealthy fellow citizens occupied 18 centuries ago. Next day the family's work-bound father may walk past the Forum on his way to the Colosseum station of the Rome subway, while the children head for the emperors' old beach at Ostia.

RELIGIOUS RELICS *of Christianity's early days lie beneath St. Peter's. Among them, by tradition, are the bones of the Apostle Peter himself*

MAUSOLEUMS of early Christians, some dating back to the Second Century, line a passage in the lower Vatican grottoes.

PORTRAIT OF A POPE, John VII (*right*), gives him a square halo to indicate the mosaic was made before he died in 707.

PAGAN SCULPTURE of glowing beauty, also found under St. Peter's, includes a satyr carrying an infant Bacchus.

THE GLORY *that was Rome, unsurpassed at its peak, was defiled, after the murder of Julius Caesar, by a voluptuous way of life and an insatiable lust for bloody games staged in huge arenas*

FALLEN CAESAR, slain in 44 B.C. by a group of conspirators led by Brutus, lies dead on the Senate floor as his followers flee the room. He had transformed the republic into a dictatorship.

RUINED COLOSSEUM (*opposite*), floodlighted and moonlit, rises near the site of Nero's palace. The columns (*foreground*) belong to Hadrian's Temple of Venus and Roma.

REIGNING EMPEROR, a Roman ruler accepts the plaudits of gladiators about to die. For three centuries the hideous crimes in the Colosseum amused the decadent Romans.

In a Raphael fresco, Constantine (center, with spear) fights a rival's forces at Milvian Bridge in 312 A.D. Inspired by a cross in t

On the Piazza del Duomo in Milan, where a good speaker always draws a crowd, a leftist orator harangues a group of passers-by. This

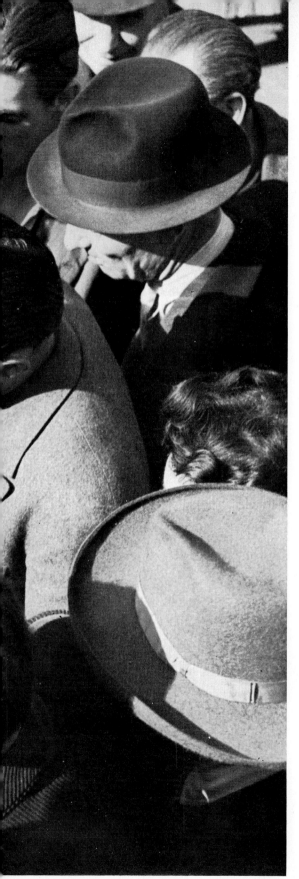

kind of fiery spirit has long imbued Italian political history

3

An Age of Dreams and Disillusion

JUST 100 years ago, a newly unified Italy burst upon the world with a glory of operatic rhetoric accompanying its *Risorgimento*, or "resurrection," as a united country. The century that followed has been filled with operatic politics and political operas, and in both cases the plots have often been complicated. As there are footnotes that shed light on a libretto, there are clues to illuminate the snarled story, if not entirely to clarify it.

The first clue is the divisiveness inherited from a turbulent past. Caught between the sea and the Alps, the Italy of the early 19th Century was an island in the European world, an island as tempestuously disunited as a basket of snakes. Italy's lands remained in parcels belonging to autonomous cities and foreign dynasties, all interested in power and the suppression of rivals. Old animosities, the parochialisms of history, were firmly rooted.

An Italian's patriotism was not love of country or nation but loyalty to tribe or commune.

The gentry and peasantry hated and feared one another and even the peasants were suspicious of each other, clinging to their various types of land tenure. Weights, measures and currencies differed everywhere, and a shipment of goods floating down the Po to the Adriatic had to pass as many as 22 different customs barriers.

The second clue lies within the Italian character. Robust, ebullient, energetic and animated, Italians have been an opera-loving people for whom the violence of the stage is as much a way of life as an art form. Cherishing the memory of the greatness they had when the young world was an open horizon, they arrived in a cynically modern world as the *innocenti* of western Europe. Strong leaders, good and bad, have understood this memory and exploited it.

In their weakness, Italians have above all admired strength. Time and time again they have fallen pell-mell behind any reasonable facsimile of a Caesar who offered the delusion of liberation, and like lemmings have plunged blindly with him into the unknown. This is the tragedy of Italian history and Italian politics.

On the surface, at least, Italy hardly changed at all during the first half of the 19th Century. Every week in Tuscany and the various provinces, ministers waited upon their princes to present their reports and submit their appeals. The same monotonous tasks were performed in Naples before King Ferdinand IV, in Lombardy and Venetia before Austrian rulers and in the Papal States before an intangible army of clerics.

BUT in subtler ways Italians had begun to identify themselves with the mainstream of European history. Napoleon's French legions had introduced not only the germs of liberal thought but an enlightened code of law and efficient methods of administering it. Italy's mercantile classes were appreciative, and many new nationalist leaders were from families who had become rich under Napoleon. They looked ahead to the large internal markets which unification might bring. All that was needed, they believed, was for Italy to rid itself of French and Austrian occupiers and papal oppressors.

The stage was set. Italy, as it had done so many times before, was waiting for leadership. In a stroke of good fortune rare in its history, it found not one man—always a dangerous arrangement for it—but three.

FIRST came the visionary and utopian Giuseppe Mazzini. Among his disciples were two men as forceful and extraordinary as himself, the activist Giuseppe Garibaldi and the statesman-strategist Count Camillo di Cavour. It was a northern triumvirate. Mazzini was a Genoese lawyer, Garibaldi a sailor born in Nice, Cavour an aristocrat from Piedmont (a region of the Kingdom of Sardinia, which consisted of Savoy, Piedmont and the island of Sardinia). What these men shared was a self-sacrificing devotion to the cause of a united Italy. Otherwise it would be hard to imagine three more dissimilar characters.

Because of the nature of their separate roles, the three leaders were complementary and indispensable to one another. Later their differences, their mistrust for each other and their proud Italian individualism sometimes moved them to work at cross purposes. But by then the miracle of unification was begun.

Through the "Young Italy" revolutionary society which he founded in 1831, Mazzini inflamed the youth of Italy with his "theory of popular initiative." According to Mazzini a nation, being something spiritual, can be united only by an uprising of ordinary people: a population must rise against tyranny on its own initiative, resolving for itself the problems of national and class selfishness. He convinced his followers that unification was a religious duty, and he dreamed that the state would be a democratic republic. Because of these radical views he was exiled from his native Genoa and from Piedmont, and then expelled from France and Switzerland. He spent most of his adult life in London, plotting his revolution. In personal life a mild, shy little man, sad and affectionate, Mazzini was one of the most feared, adored and hated personalities of his generation.

To Mazzini's great sorrow, the *Risorgimento*

never developed into the nationwide republican movement he had envisioned. Instead it was taken over by a sort of elite of the intellectually disinherited—idealistic students, lawyers, writers and scholars. The driving forces turned out to be the educated unemployed or underemployed, some of them politicians whose achievements had not equaled their ambitions.

Guiseppe Garibaldi was also an exile. After taking part in an unsuccessful revolt in the Sardinian Navy in 1834, he had fled to South America. There he corresponded with Mazzini. In 1848, the year the city-states, declaring themselves republics, rose up in the war of Italian independence against Austria, he returned to Italy. Forming a volunteer army, he set about defending the newly proclaimed Roman Republic, which under Mazzini's leadership had freed itself from papal rule. The war ended in defeat, with Italy still under the Austrian heel and the Pope restored to his temporal possessions. But now Italy had a romantic hero around whom to rally.

UNSOPHISTICATED, with little comprehension of strategy, Garibaldi possessed a peculiar genius for guerrilla warfare. In contrast to Mazzini—and Cavour—he was without guile. He abhorred ostentation and had no ambition for himself. But he understood his people, for he wrote, "I had become more and more convinced that the only way to get Italians to see eye to eye and agree with each other was by using armed force, nothing less."

His soldiers loved him and believed that he was invincible, and this was the source of his strength. He had an electrifying speaking voice which seemingly turned the most mortal of men into proud warriors. He was able to unite to his cause all the malcontents who traditionally thrive on disorder, those combustible elements forever present in Italian society. To join his troops young men came from many lands— Negroes from South America and a cabinet minister's son from England, among others.

With a thousand of his "redshirts" and a few rusty flintlocks Garibaldi landed in Sicily in 1860 and, aided by a peasant revolt, conquered a large Bourbon garrison. Moving on to occupy Naples, he established headquarters in the magnificent Palace of Caserta, washed his own shirt and slept on hay, using his saddle for a pillow. In effect he now controlled all of southern Italy. When Cavour, who was premier of Sardinia, heard of Garibaldi's successes, he sent the Sardinian Army to invade the Papal States, annexing Umbria and the Marches but cautiously avoiding Rome itself. Finally Garibaldi, who called himself a republican, was persuaded to yield his conquests to Sardinia's king in the interests of Italian unification. Thus the unification of Italy was achieved largely through the annexation of the South to the Kingdom of Sardinia.

Like Mazzini, Garibaldi became disillusioned with the nation he had helped forge with fire and blood. He distrusted Mazzini and he hated Cavour. When Cavour took over the Italian revolution Garibaldi knew his work was done. He resigned his post as deputy in Cavour's parliament, where, he said, talk and intrigue were substitutes for action, and retired for a while to the island of Caprera to write his autobiography and to campaign for a world state and universal peace. Because he was a rough, untutored man, his share in the *Risorgimento* was deprecated by officialdom. But southern Italians still venerate him as a delivering saint.

IN contrast to the simple Garibaldi, the somber, aristocratic Count Camillo di Cavour was a man of the world. He had an imperfect knowledge of Italian, preferring to write and speak in French. But he believed passionately in the ability of the Italian to govern himself. Italy and Germany were moving toward unification at the same time, and it was Cavour's conviction that Piedmont should take the same leading role in Italy as Prussia was taking in Germany. He played France against Austria to gain his ends, and used Mazzini and Garibaldi when it suited his purposes. Though wary of republicanism, he was liberal enough to insist that a constitutional monarchy was the only type of government that could reconcile liberty and order. To unite Italy he had to balance his theoretical liberalism with a practical Machiavellianism.

Within weeks after Garibaldi handed over the South to Sardinia, Cavour had unified most of the peninsula. He had already held rigged plebiscites to legitimize the act, and now at last the traditionally independent and autonomous units of the Italian peninsula began a common life as a single political entity. When a parliament representing the newly united provinces met for the first time in early 1861, a kingdom of 22 million people was officially in existence. Only Rome, under French protection, and Venice, under Austrian rule, remained as important areas outside the control of the new state.

Vittorio Emmanuele II, who since 1849 had been King of Sardinia, became King of Italy. A statue of the king in military uniform that stands in the public square of Sássari shows him a puny, absurdly Napoleonic little man. Superstitious and ill educated, he nevertheless had a good-natured character without royal pretensions. His passions were reserved for military reviews, horses, hunting and women.

The premiership was an office not mentioned in the new Italian constitution, but Cavour, by the strength of his own leadership, made it all-important. Unfortunately Cavour died when the kingdom was only five months old. In his absence the old prejudices and animosities quickly cast their shadows over the new government.

AFTER the first few years, politicians tended to polarize into two factions, conservative and radical, a division which has remained in Italian politics to date. But these have been generalized categories marking only the rough division of deputies into vague groups without fixed compositions and principles. Frequent coalitions among them have obscured the basic distinctions. Furthermore, government leaders have been too independent in their views to enable a disciplined party system to operate.

Instead of functioning within the framework of a two-party system, Italian ministers have based their power on alliances formed from an amorphous majority ranging over the spectrum of the parties. These majority groups are usually made up of deputies who have a common political-economic interest, or who come from similar geographic regions, rather than of members of a single party. Governments are forever being modified. In the first 35 years of the new nation Italy had 33 different cabinets, and during one of these crises Journalist Ferdinando Petrucelli wrote, "A gust of wind and these leaves which call themselves deputies will be blown about and mixed up anew."

FROM 1861 to 1865, the years of the American Civil War, there was also a "civil war" between the North and South in Italy. Naples, which had so recently rebelled against Bourbon misgovernment, now chafed under the "colonial" rule of the North. Highly unpopular northern "carpetbaggers" were frequently laid upon by brigands. The war was partly an insurrection in the South and partly a northern campaign of retaliation against the brigandage which was a southern way of life. Brigands had long been regarded in the South as champions of the peasants in their struggle against the landlords, and they were even accepted as allies by the Church and the unseated Bourbons.

The government sent an army of 120,000 into the South. When the civil war was over it was found that the number of people who had died in it was greater than the total number killed in the wars of the *Risorgimento*. Brigandage survived and flourished. In Sicily it was personified in the Mafia, a group of gangs which extorted protection money and presided over smuggling and kidnaping activity; in Naples it was manifested in the Camorra, which specialized in intimidation and blackmail, had its own police force and courts of justice and sometimes placed its own deputies in the parliament.

Although the South was subdued, the *Risorgimento* had yet to incorporate Austrian and papal enclaves still existing on the peninsula. In 1866 Venice was presented to Italy as a gift by Prussia, its ally in a war against Austria. But Rome proved a more nettlesome problem. The new republic's hostility to the papacy was based not only on the fact that the Pope still held the Eternal City—which Cavour had declared *must* be the capital of Italy—but also on the papacy's historical opposition to Italian unification. In 1862 and 1867 Garibaldi and his red shirts, shouting "Rome or death!" had tried to capture the city, but each time they were betrayed by the new Italian government, when it tardily realized the strength of France's opposition.

Anticlerical sentiment meanwhile had led to the confiscation of vast Church landholdings, and many religious orders had been forced to disband. In 1870, while France was preoccupied by its fateful war with Prussia, Italy was able to seize the weakly defended city. Rome became the capital of Italy, and the Pope lost his temporal powers. The result was the beginning of a long, destructive struggle between the Vatican and the king's residence, the Quirinale. The Pope rejected the generous compensations proffered him by the government, refused to recognize the existence of the Italian state and voluntarily "imprisoned" himself in the Vatican.

NOT only was Rome handicapped by the Vatican's rivalry, but the kingdom which it governed faced tremendous problems. Italy was still an agricultural and peasant land. Sicily, once the granary of old Rome, was no longer able to feed itself. Swamps bred mosquitoes. Even after the *Risorgimento*, five million acres of forests were destroyed and rivers continued to wash topsoil into the sea. Landslides and earthquakes were frequent. Brigandage and crime flourished and the populace remained predominantly illiterate. Meanwhile a distrust of modernism kept investment capital out of industry. Deficient in raw materials and unable to afford machinery from abroad, the country found itself left out of the industrial revolution that was transforming the rest of Europe.

Yet the Italian laborer was one of the hardest-working in the world, and because there was insufficient employment at home he traveled to other countries to help build the Suez Canal, the harbors of Calais and Marseilles and the railroads and cities of America.

Though beset by severe problems at home, Italy now adopted an imperialist policy abroad. "Italy must not only be respected, she must make herself feared," Vittorio Emmanuele proclaimed. In 1878 the monarch died of malaria. His son, Umberto I, set up a royal household grand enough to outshine the Vatican, and his queen, Margherita, became the leader of society. In 1882, piqued by France's annexation of Tunisia, a country which Italians had long coveted, Italy joined Prussia and Austria in concluding the so-called Triple Alliance.

Soon the nation embarked on a ruinous race for armaments, colonies and prestige. It was under the iron rule of the proud and pathologically sensitive Sicilian premier, Francesco Crispi, that Italy foolishly started a tariff war with France which bankrupted its own economy. Undaunted, Crispi decided that only the conquest of Ethiopia would free Italy from its "imprisonment in the Mediterranean," fulfill its "mission" in Africa and, incidentally, detract attention from the corrupt nature of his regime. A badly mismanaged military campaign resulted in a humiliating defeat at Aduwa in 1896. Italy was stunned and Crispi fell from power.

FOUR years later, in 1900, the unpopular Umberto was assassinated by an anarchist who had returned from the United States to kill him. A year later Giuseppe Verdi, whose operatic assassinations were spattering make-believe blood over the stages of Europe and America, died in Milan. The two deaths ended an era of real and fictional violence in Italy and marked the beginning of a period of tranquillity, a lull before the storm. The death of Verdi was commemorated in a small-town theater with a speech by a young student named Benito Mussolini.

Vittorio Emmanuele III was a soberer king than his father. Delicate, with a frail body and an inferiority complex, he preferred to live in his private house rather than the royal palace. His queen, the daughter of a Montenegrin chieftain, liked to prepare the family meals herself and was referred to by one of her husband's royal relatives as "my cousin, the shepherdess."

The new king was fortunate in having at his side a reformer from Piedmont, Giovanni Giolitti, who served as premier for most of the period between 1901 and 1914. Giolitti's most notable achievement was his attempt to meet the growing social unrest in Italy with concessions rather than repression. He believed that Italy could achieve stability only by giving the working class a greater stake in the nation's prosperity. Unlike his predecessors, he encouraged labor unions instead of persecuting them. He greatly extended the franchise and thereby made way for the new mass parties (Socialist, Fascist and Church-backed) which were to develop. Italy prospered. Foreign trade doubled between 1900 and 1910, wages rose and the general standard of living improved.

Even the southern question for the moment became less acute—not because conditions in the South had improved very much, but because surplus agricultural labor was now emigrating.

In 1913 alone, 872,000 people, largely young adult males, left Italy. Most of them were drawn to the United States by the prospect of high wages and by the seemingly endless capacity of American industry to absorb extra manpower.

In 1912 Italian morale was boosted at last by colonial success. A year-long war in Libya against the Turks and the Arabs ended in an Italian victory and the establishment of a ministry of colonies. But while it gave Italy a toe hold in Africa, the triumph was an expensive one. Capital was needed to develop the new colony, and Italy did not even have enough to develop its own land.

When World War I broke out in 1914, Italy declared its neutrality. But as the conflict went on, many Italians began to think of neutrality as undignified. The blood memory of the Caesars stirred in them. They began to wonder: Wasn't war the means to national greatness?

So in April 1915, Premier Antonio Salandra

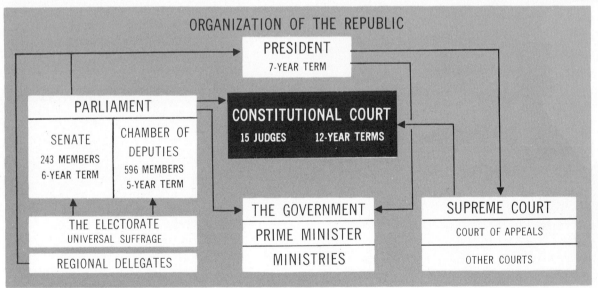

ITALY'S CENTRAL GOVERNMENT under the 1947 constitution is like that of the U.S. in having three branches: legislative, executive and judicial. The president is elected by Parliament and by delegates from the country's 19 regions. He picks the Government (prime minister and other ministers). The Government is responsible to Parliament, from which most ministers are recruited. The president is also chairman of the Supreme Court, the highest judicial body, whose members are chosen by Parliament and other judges. The president, Parliament and the Supreme Court all nominate members of the Constitutional Court, an independent body with wide powers of review. The Constitutional Court also rules on any impeachment of the president.

Local government consists of regions, provinces and communes. Each is ruled by an elected council which chooses an executive junta and a chief executive (regions and provinces have presidents, communes have mayors).

concluded the secret Treaty of London, committing Italy to go to war on the side of England and France and against its former allies, Germany and Austria. The nationalist poet Gabriele D'Annunzio was recalled from France—to which he had fled to escape some heavy debts—and with an operatic flourish he declaimed on the Capitoline Hill: "Our genius demands that we should put our stamp on the molten metal of the new world." In the parliament, deputies hoarsely shouted, "Long live the war!"

THE war turned out to be much longer than they expected. And despite the fact that a victorious peace gave Italy Trieste and some 9,000 square miles of former Austro-Hungarian territory, the country suffered badly from the conflict, emerging from it in a state of economic collapse. By 1922 the political situation had become so confused and tempers so inflamed that revolvers were brandished in the parliament. Once again Italians, as they had so frequently in the past, sought a strong deliverer to lead them out of the chaos. And this time they had the bad luck to find one who had exactly the talent, allure and lack of principle to exploit their predicament. He was Benito Mussolini.

As early as 1912, at a Socialist congress, Mussolini, then 28, had scored a roaring oratorical success shouting for class revolution. He was a peasant from Romagna, a traditionally left-wing area. His father, a Socialist blacksmith, had named him for the Mexican revolutionary, Benito Juárez. Mussolini in 1914 broke with the Socialists and began organizing an anti-Socialist, antidemocratic movement, fascism. Mussolini's early followers were the same types of idealists, students, unemployed white-collar workers, extreme nationalists, veterans and adventurers that had supported Mazzini and Garibaldi. The imaginations of these malcontents were inflamed in 1919 by the poet D'Annunzio, who led a shouting mob on an invasion of the Adriatic port of Fiume, coveted by both Italy and Yugoslavia. The comic-opera occupation came to an ignominious end after one year when D'Annunzio's followers, weakened by an epidemic of Spanish influenza, surrendered to the Italian government at the first show of force. It served nonetheless as a roistering dress rehearsal for Italian fascism.

Mussolini's opportunity came with the advent of industrial, railroad and postal strikes in 1920 and 1921. When the government showed that it was unable to cope with the crisis, the rabble-rouser suddenly found himself a figure of national importance. In the elections of 1921, thanks to an alliance with more respectable parties, the Fascists won 35 parliamentary seats.

Support from every level of society gathered around the new Caesar and his blackshirted cohorts. Men of property—bankers and industrialists—wanted a strong central government to control labor and tariffs. The lower middle class, strong now in the big northern cities, hoped for a means of controlling postwar inflation. Catholics looked upon the Fascists as a defense against the Bolshevik atheism which was threatening the world from Moscow.

The king, an apathetic swimmer-with-the-tide, worried that if he opposed the Fascists they would depose him. In October 1922 he refused to sign a cabinet decree ordering Italy's army to suppress a threatened blackshirt "march on Rome." Instead he sent a telegram inviting the new Caesar to come to Rome to form a ministry. Mussolini's famous "march" was actually a comfortable train ride in a sleeping car from Milan, followed by the straggling arrival of 25,000 largely unarmed blackshirts, all with the blessing of the king. But this time the comic opera had suddenly turned dead serious. Benito Mussolini, *Il Duce* (the leader), was at 39 the youngest premier in modern Italian history.

TO entrench his position, Mussolini pushed through the parliament the Acerbo Law, which gave an automatic parliamentary majority and two thirds of the deputies' seats to the party winning the largest number of votes in a national election, provided this was at least 25 per cent of the total votes cast. With this notorious act Italy's parliamentarians cleared the way for the destruction of the country's democratic constitution. In the first nationwide election under Mussolini, the Fascists won 65 per cent of the vote.

The tragic farce rolled on, faithfully following the libretto. Rational men either fled or were silenced at home. Giacomo Matteotti, a Socialist who had dared to criticize Mussolini in parliament, was murdered by Fascist thugs. Italy was scandalized, but the anti-Fascist members of the parliament were too disunited to take advantage of Mussolini's tarnished popularity, and the king closed his eyes to all evil.

IN 1925 Mussolini formally assumed dictatorial powers, and the last non-Fascist ministers meekly resigned from his cabinet. "The crowd loves a strong man," Mussolini loved to say. "The crowd is like a woman." So he produced himself in public, a swaggering braggadocio. Guarded from his adoring followers were the facts of his eyeglasses, his ulcer and various unglamorous diseases.

In 1929, Pope Pius XI emerged from the Vatican for a reconciliation with "the man sent us by Providence." The Lateran Treaty was signed, giving the Pope complete authority over the newly independent state of the Vatican. Mussolini, at the apex of his career, was widely praised for having resolved the long-standing feud between church and state.

To compensate for fascism's lack of constructive purpose, Mussolini proudly created a "corporate state," which he boasted was an alternative to both capitalism and communism. Borrowing freely from the ideas of others, he established a huge bureaucracy of "corporations" composed of employers and employees in various branches of the economy. The corporation sent deputies to the rubber-stamp parliament and served as instruments of government control over economic life.

Mussolini's economic goal was to make Italy self-sufficient. He gave medals to farmers for raising more wheat (which cost half again as much as American wheat), but one of the main consequences was that the production of wine, fruit and olive oil fell. The drop in emigration (the U.S. Immigration Law of 1921 cut Italy's annual quota drastically) had badly compounded the country's overpopulation problem, but Mussolini subsidized matrimony and launched a "battle for births."

With his domestic reforms mostly failures, the Duce in the early 1930s started looking beyond Italy's borders. A virile people, he said, "has the right to empire." He had been planning for years to invade Ethiopia, and although English and French diplomats secretly offered to give him part of the country, he insisted on conquering it militarily. Proclaiming Italy the victim of "unprovoked aggression" by Ethiopia, Mussolini attacked in October 1935. The League of Nations imposed token sanctions.

The fall of Ethiopia's capital, Addis Ababa, after seven months of frail resistance, gave the Duce the fatal euphoria of overconfidence. He was extolled by the Italian king for winning "the greatest colonial war ever recorded in history." Many years later the Pagliaccio of politics was to say that he wished his ulcer had killed him at that moment.

THE League sanctions and Europe's refusal to recognize Italy's Ethiopian empire propelled the Duce into an alliance with Germany's new dictator, Adolf Hitler. At first Mussolini clung to the illusion that he was the senior partner. During the 1920s, he said, Hitler had adopted *his* Roman salute, and the title of "Führer" had been copied from "Duce." But Hitler was soon to surpass him. As Italy's great philosopher Benedetto Croce pointed out, there was a revealing difference between Hitler and Mussolini: "The first had a tragic and diabolical aspect, but the second kept an incorrigible clownlike appearance." While Hitler was proving successful in the realization of his evil purposes, Mussolini, eaten from within by jealousy, was degenerating both physically and mentally.

The Duce in 1936 made the mistake of intervening with Hitler in Spain, to help General Francisco Franco in a civil war that was to continue for three years. This drained off important military strength from Italy, but early in 1939, piqued at Hitler for not forewarning him about the German invasion of Czechoslovakia, Mussolini marched into Albania.

Before continuing his conquests, the Duce planned to spend a few years putting Italy's industry and armed forces on a wartime footing. But a month after Hitler attacked Poland in September of 1939 and began World War II, Mussolini confided to his son-in-law, Count Galeazzo Ciano, that he was envious of Hitler's glory, and the following June he declared war on France and England. He started hostilities with a farcical march against the French, whom the Germans had already defeated, and followed this with an African campaign in which he was soon routed by the British.

Again, spurred by Hitler's victories, Mussolini attacked Greece, and this proved to be the greatest national disaster in the history of modern Italy. In a few weeks the army was in full and tragicomic retreat. German troops had to come to the rescue of the Italians in both Africa and the Balkans. Eventually the infuriated Germans were even forced to occupy Italy itself.

When the Allies invaded Sicily in June 1943 the opposition to Mussolini within Italy finally coalesced. That July the Grand Council of Fascism voted no confidence in Mussolini. The king had the Duce arrested and appointed Marshal Pietro Badoglio premier. Badoglio and Italy's new "nonpolitical" government made secret overtures of peace to the Allies and signed an armistice early in September. But German troops held all of Italy north of Naples in their grip, and German paratroopers daringly rescued Mussolini from confinement, setting him up as the head of a "republican-Fascist" government at Salò in northern Italy.

IN October 1944 Italy formally declared war on Germany, and the Allies, aided by Italian partisans, gradually pushed the Germans back up the peninsula. The following April a band of partisans captured Mussolini and his mistress near Lake Como and summarily executed them. Their bodies were later strung up by the heels outside a gas station in Milan. It was Italy's traditional—and, incidentally, extremely operatic—method of dealing with a fallen hero.

With Germany's surrender in May 1945 the war in Europe was over. Alcide De Gasperi, the ablest Italian statesman since Cavour, became premier that December. The following June the Italian people voted by a narrow margin to declare Italy a republic, and its last king, Umberto II, abdicated after a reign of only 34 days. Italy's first postwar elections, held in April 1948, gave a huge majority to Premier De Gasperi's Christian Democrats, and De Gasperi himself remained in office until his death in 1953.

His Vatican-supported party has continued in power ever since. During the Christian Democrats' long rule, Rome, playing its dual role as the capital of both the Italian state and world Catholicism, has flourished as the largest city in the land. The long-hostile relationship between the Quirinale Palace and the Vatican has become more cordial with each popular pope. Though his temporal ruling powers are limited to the Vatican's 108.7 acres, the Pope exercises moral leadership of 528 million people and is a pillar of moral force in the struggle against international communism.

THE ebullient Italians, with their sturdy national virtues of imagination, humor and willingness to work, had the country functioning again very soon after the war. There followed a period of astonishing reconstruction, generously spurred by American aid. The greatest foreign gift was the eradication of the centuries-old scourge of malaria. Especially in the South and on the islands, Italy is today a Lazarus land, its people restored from chronic sickness to increasing health. New industries in the North, oil refineries in many regions and more than 16 million tourists a year—all promise a new prosperity. In the communicative arts of literature and movie-making, a new generation of articulate talent has gathered in Rome. Through the new *realismo* of novels and motion pictures, Italy has won the respect and esteem of the world, an esteem which it tried long and vainly to attain through political means.

Young State, Ancient Church

The transformation of Italy from a mélange of petty kingdoms and Papal States into a nation was wrought by three disparate men who shared only patriotism and a compelling dream. Shy Giuseppe Mazzini inspired others by the written word. Aristocratic Camillo di Cavour was born to statesmanship. Unlettered Giuseppe Garibaldi was a skilled warrior. Their alliance ended in bitterness, and in the ensuing century their work was almost undone and Italy was almost destroyed by the pompous Benito Mussolini. Ironically, however, Mussolini did help settle one of Italy's thorniest problems: that of the Vatican, shown on the following pages.

MAZZINI, a writer, made the establishment of an Italian republic his life's mission.

CAVOUR, nobleman of Piedmont, attempted to reconcile liberalism with monarchism.

GARIBALDI, a guileless sailor and soldier (*opposite*), concerned himself chiefly with Italy's liberation, and though calling himself a republican, he bowed to the monarchy.

MUSSOLINI, a onetime journalist and Socialist, fancied himself a latter-day Caesar and delighted in such military rituals as this dagger salute by his soldiers in Rome.

INDEPENDENT STATUS for the Vatican was finally granted by the Lateran Treaty, signed in 1929 by Papal Secretary of State Gasparri (*center*) and Premier Mussolini (*right*).

THE VATICAN, *tiniest of the world's sovereign states, is the heart of Christendom's most potent spiritual domain*

DOMED ST. PETER'S, largest of all churches, dominates the 108.7-acre Vatican. To the left of the dome is the peak-roofed Sistine Chapel and beyond is St. Peter's Square.

POPE JOHN XXIII (*opposite*), shown receiving homage shortly after his election in 1958, is St. Peter's 261st successor. Under him the Vatican has been more informal.

DEATH OF A POPE, an event that saddens many millions, is attended by ceremonials showing the Roman Catholic Church at its most majestic. In this historic photograph Pope Pius XII, who died in 1958, lies in state in St. Peter's, a high miter on his head, tall candles burning by his catafalque. He had been head of the Church 19 years.

CROWNING OF A POPE (*below*) attracts a multitude to St. Peter's Square as John XXIII is elevated in 1958. The great open space, forever abustle with visitors, is framed by the massive 17th Century colonnades of Bernini, built during Pope Alexander VII's reign. The papal apartments are on the top floor of the building at the extreme right.

SPLENDOR of St. Peter's (*opposite*) attains its peak when a pope ascends his throne for ceremonies like the bestowal of new cardinals' red hats in 1953.

SIMPLICITY of a country convent is revealed at Assisi, where devotees march in honor of St. Clare. A friend of St. Francis, she founded the Poor Clares.

Seen through the statue-topped spires of Milan's sumptuous late Gothic cathedral, new skyscrapers rise dramatically over the economic

The North: Land of Prosperity

capital of Italy. In the left background is the glass-sheathed Galfa Building; second from right is the Pirelli Building, Italy's tallest.

EACH morning in the Milan railroad station a poignant scene demonstrates the extent to which Italy, for all its seeming unity, is still a nation of deep and tragic divisions.

On one track, first-class sleeping cars, just rolled in from Switzerland's Gotthard Pass, are unloading night-traveling Milanese returning from business trips to the commercial and banking cities of northern Europe—Zurich, Brussels, London and Amsterdam. The self-assured international businessmen, shaved and fresh in blue national businessmen, shaved and fresh in blue or gray pin-striped suits and accompanied by chic women in furs and tweeds, walk briskly behind porters out of the terminal.

On another track, at the same moment, ill-smelling coaches from Italy's South are letting out travel-weary Sicilians and Calabrians. Short, dark men wearing green moleskin suits peer worriedly about the station, looking for a relative or an old friend. The women, unslept and frightened, wearing black shawls and skirts and clutching cloth bundles and cardboard suitcases, huddle in protective coveys around their thin, grave children, who are absorbing with wide eyes the bustle and confusion.

The passing Milanese businessmen cast distasteful glances at these intruders, whom they call *terruni*, from the Italian *terra*, or earth. The invaders average 115 a day, and some Milanese, who have only two or three children to a family, fear that the prolific *terruni* may some day breed them out of existence. Already Sicilians control the city's fruit and vegetable markets and Neapolitans the retail textile business. The city is ringed as in a besiegement with a shantytown belt of 200,000 of the newcomers.

Outside the railroad station the newly arrived *terruni* face an astonishing sight. They might even think for a moment that they have died and have been resurrected in a 20th Century materialistic paradise—one that they recognize from having seen it in the movies. There are a dozen skyscrapers, one of them 33 stories tall, and the streets are a jam-pack of fast-moving autos (Milan has 450,000 licensed vehicles).

Where is the border that the *terruni* cross on their flight from South to North? Italy's Mason-Dixon Line is roughly the old boundary between the Bourbon kingdom to the south and the Papal States to the north. It begins near Rome at a point below the 42nd parallel, and runs northeast to the Adriatic below Ancona, at the 44th parallel. This division, adopted by postwar government reconstruction agencies in their official reckonings, places in the North what was traditionally a central area made up of Tuscany and the Papal States.

TODAY the North is the seat of Italy's amazing postwar industrial boom. Though many tourists are unaware of it, this prosperous region holds the key to the country's progress and new-found economic wealth. It contains 57 per cent of Italy's land and 60 per cent of its population. Of the country's 10 major cities, all but Naples and Palermo are in the North. The economic flowering centers on a triumvirate of northern cities: manufacturing Turin, banking and shipping Genoa and commercial Milan.

Milan is the leader. Paced by the achievements of this one city, Italy today has the third largest industrial production in Europe. The advance has come about in a country which is basically agricultural, whose land is limited, whose store of minerals and raw materials is insufficient and which has hardly enough food for its own people.

THE change has been accomplished in part by the natural resource which has always been Italy's greatest: its people. A number of brilliant industrial leaders have used modern techniques to build highly successful manufacturing corporations, and they have been aided in their efforts by the country's improving labor force. There has been an increase in the ranks of labor, owing to Italy's postwar baby boom, to a lowering of the death rate and to a decrease in opportunities for emigration, and this has continued the heavy burden of unemployment in the country. But at the same time there has been an increase in skilled labor, which the tycoons have taken advantage of to build plants and factories equal in efficiency to any in the West.

Milan's prosperity, however, is a historical tradition. In the Second Century B.C., the Romans captured from the Gauls the strategic settlement of Mediolanum, located at a point in the wild Po River lands where the main road from Rome split into roads leading to Alpine passes. The Romans were aware also of the vast agricultural potentiality of the fertile plains.

During the Middle Ages, while Rome was in a decline, Mediolanum—today's Milan—was developing into Europe's wool capital, and by the 14th Century, 70 woolen mills in Milan were employing 60,000 workers. Merchants arrived from all over northern Europe to buy textiles, silk, glassware and arms, and the Lombard bankers were among the most important in Europe.

During the century since Italy's unification the Milanese, scarcely impeded by wars, have increased both the quantity and the diversity of their products. Today the region in which Milan is located, Lombardy, has 112 industries employing 1,300,000 persons, about a third of all the factory workers in Italy. The per capita annual income in the province of Milan is more than $600—more than twice the Italian national average and six times that of the poorest province in the South, Potenza. About a quarter of Italy's share capital is concentrated in Milan.

Milan's affluent residents, aware that they constitute less than four per cent of Italy's 50 million people but pay 26 per cent of the nation's tax bill, often like to speculate how much more fortunate they would be if Lombardy were a canton of neighboring Switzerland, instead of being tied to the dragging weight of southern Italy. A University of Rome economic geographer, Professor Ferdinando Milone, has said, "If by some strange chance Lombardy's industry were to stop, the whole of Italian industry, or almost, would come to a halt, paralyzing the nation's life."

MOST of Italian industry as a whole falls into a few basic categories. The first, because of the booming auto business, is engineering, which besides car manufacturing includes electrical supplies and agricultural machinery, along with shipbuilding and aircraft, both of them ailing since the war. A second category is the building industry. Another is chemicals, in which 200,000 men are employed to produce basic compounds, as well as dyes, fertilizers and explosives. Still others are ceramics and glass, an old craft largely in the hands of artisans; food processing, especially *pasta* and tomato paste for export; electric power, and motion pictures, a postwar industry which is now second only to that in the United States.

The success of these enterprises must be credited in great part to an amazing generation of industrial geniuses. The first of these was Giovanni Agnelli, the Henry Ford of Italy, co-founder in 1899 of the Fiat auto company and manager of that vast empire until his death in 1945. Probably the best known have been Camillo and Adriano Olivetti, father and son, typewriter manufacturers who by their worker welfare programs have become the patron saints of Italian industry. By the time Adriano died in

1959 he had expanded the firm to first place among Europe's business-machine manufacturers, and his company had such a strong financial position that it was able in early 1960 to surprise American industry by buying out one of the most hallowed firms in the U.S., the Underwood Typewriter Company. Another entrepreneur is Enrico Piaggio, who after World War II converted his family's bomb-wrecked airplane factories to the production of Vespa (literally "wasp") motor scooters, starting a revolution not only in industry but in Italian life.

Not all of Italy's business is privately owned. The country has more government-controlled enterprises than any European state outside the Iron Curtain. The state mines all Italy's coal and most of its iron, has a monopoly of rail, sea and air transportation and competes with private industry in the manufacture of a host of products, from chocolates to Alfa Romeo luxury cars. Two huge corporations, autonomous in administration but responsible to the state like America's Tennessee Valley Authority or England's London Port Authority, dominate the field of government industry.

The first corporation, the Institute for Industrial Reconstruction (IRI), was founded in 1933. Its purpose, something like that of America's Reconstruction Finance Corporation, was to rescue banks from collapse. But it has expanded into telephones, shipping, steel, electricity, radio and television. The second state institution, the National Hydrocarbons Agency (ENI), was founded by businessman Enrico Mattei after he discovered natural gas in the Po Valley in 1946 and obtained from Parliament a monopoly on the development of hydrocarbon deposits. It has since mushroomed into oil refining, shipping, mining, pipelines, motel chains, synthetic rubber and, finally, nuclear power.

IN all industrial Europe, Italy has the widest extremes of living standards, and the successful citizen of Milan is at the top of the heap. In the casinos of San Remo and Monte Carlo he is one of the freest gamblers. He summers at the Ligurian coast resorts of Santa Margherita,

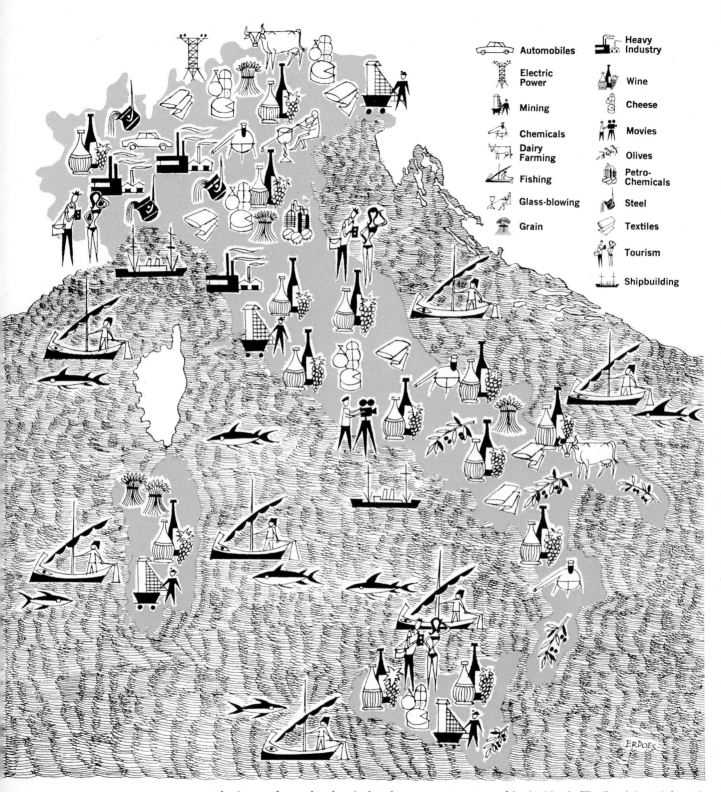

Legend:

- Automobiles
- Electric Power
- Mining
- Chemicals
- Dairy Farming
- Fishing
- Glass-blowing
- Grain
- Heavy Industry
- Wine
- Cheese
- Movies
- Olives
- Petro-Chemicals
- Steel
- Textiles
- Tourism
- Shipbuilding

ERDOES

ITALY'S PRODUCTS, both manufactured and agricultural, are shown on the map above. Heavy industry and allied activities, like steelmaking and automobile production, are concentrated in the North. The South is mainly agricultural, though its land is poorer than that of the North. Tourism and winemaking flourish in all parts of Italy.

Portofino and Rapallo, and his yacht is both a status symbol and a tax dodge.

Even the northern laborer is better off than his counterpart elsewhere in Italy. Look down from the balcony of a bright new apartment house built by the Fiat auto company in Turin, and you will see the rolling green court of a company sports club where workers are playing *bocce*, or Italian bowls. A block away is the company medical center, the most modern of its kind in Italy, and near it is a company nursery. Beyond is the neighborhood church with its company-financed youth recreation center. What you are looking at is a little Fiat world, equipped to fulfill a worker's every need.

AN idea of how the Fiat worker lives can be got by visiting the three-room plus bath and kitchen apartment of Antonio Tarasco, his wife Ines and their two sons and daughter. A slight, work-worn mechanic who is the son of a Piedmont farmer, Antonio at 49 has worked in Fiat's iron shop for 24 years. His monthly salary of $160, plus Christmas bonus and other benefits, makes him one of Italy's "workers de luxe": Fiat workers earn an average of 80 per cent more than the Italian minimum-wage scale.

On his 25th anniversary with Fiat, Antonio will join the "Fiat Elders" and receive a bonus of $200. A "collaboration prize" for workers who do not go out on strike amounts to about $60 annually and has become an expected part of the year's salary. Antonio and Ines once used theirs to buy their first wrist watches.

Ines Tarasco, who used to deposit her children in company nurseries while she worked, now spends all her time managing the home and the family economy. Balancing the budget has been made pleasanter by the older son, Albino, 20, who works as a plumber and dutifully turns his monthly pay of some $50 over to his mother. She returns $12 to him so he may take his girl dancing. The second son, Giovanni, 17, is first in his class at the Fiat apprentice school, from which he may enter the company as a specialized workman.

More than half of the Tarasco budget goes for food. *Pasta* and lentils are the staple items in the diet of most Italian workers, and so the Tarascos, who eat meat every day, are unusual. Conservative churchgoers who save their money and have no "family entertainment" item in the budget, the Tarascos still lead a lively life. Antonio plays cards and *bocce* with other workers, and Ines is active in church work. Giovanni plays drums in a Fiat jazz orchestra, and Albino races his bicycle for the Fiat Sport Club. Daughter Katerina, 10, spends a month each summer at a company seaside or mountain camp.

Many of the company's employees buy luxuries on the installment plan from Fiat, which gives them a discount. But Antonio is wary of installment buying, and he put his foot down when Ines requested a refrigerator and Albino began to talk of a car. As for television, Antonio says, "It might bring in the neighbors."

BUT there are precious few workers—only 150,000 of them, or less than four per cent of Italy's factory workers—whose families come close to matching the Tarasco way of life. Antonio, who does not even belong to a company union, appears to be quite impervious to the blandishments of the Communist party. Gesticulating around his apartment, he says, "My politics are here." Fiat's progressive employee-relations policy has paid off: in the last shop elections, Communist unions captured only 21.8 per cent of the votes.

Italy does, however, have the largest Communist party west of the Iron Curtain, and nearly half of all union members are in Communist unions. It is one of Italy's complexities that Communist strength developed not in the impoverished South, but in the booming industrial cities and centers of learning in the North. Turin and Genoa have had Communist mayors. Bologna, seat of Italy's most famous university, has had a Communist government since 1945.

Although Italy's Communist leaders pay faithful allegiance to Moscow, the party has in actual practice shown no real community of purpose with Soviet or international Communist aims. It has been mainly a protest movement against the power-entrenched, Vatican-supported Christian Democrats. As such it is rooted in the 19th Century's anti-clerical movement, a tradition which can be traced back ultimately to the antipapacy Ghibellines of the Middle Ages, and which has its origins in the Italian North.

Lombardy is one of Europe's most densely populated industrial areas (770 people per square mile), but it is also the center of Italy's best farming region. Even Lombardy's unamiably dripping weather (200 days of precipitation a year) is a blessing, for it provides the only dependable moisture in Italy.

"Such is the fertility of this country," wrote the English traveler Thomas Coryate in 1608, "that I thinke no Region or Province under the Sunne may compare with it. . . . For as Italy is the garden of the world, so is Lombardy the garden of Italy. . . . The first view thereof did even refollicate my spirits and tickle my senses with inward joy."

LUCKY North! Only 23 per cent of Italy's lands are both flat and fertile, and most of the favorable terrain lies along the Po River in Lombardy, Emilia-Romagna and Venetia. The wealth of these plains is not entirely a bounty of nature but a creation of centuries of human exertion, of draining, irrigating and fertilizing. Northern crops are herbaceous (as compared with the tree crops of the South) and include wheat, rice, corn, oats, sugar beets and vegetables. Cotton and flax grow in the Po delta, and cattle are raised throughout the valley.

In agriculture as well as in industry, the government is an entrepreneur, operating "Colonization Centers" in the irrigated rice paddies and the sugar-beet fields of the Po delta and also in the South. In most of these centers the farmers occupy pleasant white houses, each in its own neat plot of 10 or 12 acres. Though he lives in a separate house, the young farmer, like Antonio Tarasco at Fiat, lives a cooperative life centered in a village that consists of public buildings, stores, service and crop-storage depots, a church, a post office, medical clinics and community schools. The government teaches him tractor driving and his wife takes sewing lessons at a community center. Experts even tell him how and sometimes what to plant.

Despite these advantages, the young farmers have on occasion been laggard in meeting the small payments which they must make to the government for their land. A land reform official has said, "The peasant entered his new house and was unhappy because he didn't find a pot of chicken on the stove." Meanwhile there have been outbursts of Communist activity among farm laborers on some of the large land holdings that still remain in the North.

IN both agriculture and industry it must be said that the Italian "boom," so impressive to the world, has not reached Italy's full expanse of humanity. In the Po's Colonization Centers 5,617 farmers have been settled, a fraction of one per cent of the North's total agricultural workers. The farther south one travels from the Po, the unhappier the general picture grows. In a belt of mountainous country running through parts of Umbria, Tuscany and the Marches, the abandonment of thousands of sharecroppers' farms, the closing of lignite mines and the cutting back of steel output after World War II have caused the region to be classed as a depressed area. The provinces of Grosseto, Terni, Perugia and Siena have fallen in income scale. Communist-governed Spoleto, the setting for an American initiated arts festival, had 8,000 industrial workers in 1952; eight years later it had jobs for less than 3,000.

"Booming" Italy has one of the lowest per capita incomes in western Europe, and its unemployment (around 1.5 million) is the highest. So is its underemployment—about two million persons do not hold full-time jobs. Since many Italian laborers, especially the *terruni* from the South, are unskilled, the trend toward increased mechanization in both industry and agriculture can be expected to increase the unemployment. Italy's problem, then, is not, like America's or Germany's, how to humanize industrialism. It is how to bring the advantages of industrialization to the land of humanism.

In Milan's rain-washed Piazza del Duomo, a monument to Vittorio Emmanuele II rises against the glow of signs above the arched Portici

New Vigor Bestirring the North

"Milan," the Milanese boast, "is Italy's capital—for work." The northern city was the adopted home —and it is today the shrine—of Leonardo da Vinci, genius of the Renaissance. But it is, as well, the heart of another Renaissance embracing Genoa, Turin and most of Italy's North. This new Renaissance is transforming Italy into an important industrial and exporting power. It is also drawing to the cities many poverty-stricken farm laborers and transforming them into better-housed, better-fed factory workers who, happily, can afford to buy the things they produce.

THE ECONOMY'S TRANSITION *to new ways owes much of its recent impetus to American aid and to the use of formerly neglected sources of power. But many industries still require manual labor*

FAT WHEELS OF CHEESE are stacked by hand in an old factory at Corteleone, near Lodi. Cheese, made in traditional ways, forms a favorite part of every Italian meal.

VOLCANIC POWER (*opposite*) produces electricity at Larderello, in the area where spouting steam inspired Dante's vision of the Inferno. U.S. aid rebuilt the plant.

ELITE WORKERS *like Antonio Tarasco at the Fiat auto plant in Turin get good pay, superior housing and other amenities. But they are a favored minority among Italy's four million factory laborers*

ELDEST SON in the Tarasco family, 20-year-old Albino prepares to race his bicycle at the Fiat Sport Center, whose insignia he wears.

FAMILY BREADWINNER Antonio Tarasco, the son of a sharecropper, earns $160 monthly as a skilled mechanic. He has worked for Fiat for 24 years.

APPRENTICE who attends a Fiat school, Giovanni Tarasco, 17, plays with a band of fellow students. Weekly installments cost him $1.20 for his drums.

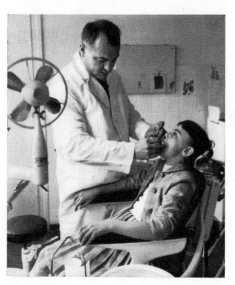

FREE CHECKUP is given to Katerina, Antonio's 10-year-old daughter, by a dentist at one of the 21 health centers organized by the Fiat medical plan.

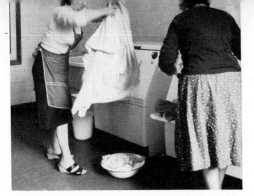

WASHDAY comes only once a week for Mrs. Tarasco (*left*), now that she can use a washing machine provided for tenants of her building.

FAMILY TIES *are generally close in Italy, and for the Tarascos a warm home life and devotion to the Church make the bond even stronger*

SUNDAY DINNER, attended by the entire family, provides ham, two other kinds of meat, spaghetti, fruit and cheese, plus a bottle of red wine donated by Antonio's father.

SUNDAY WORSHIP (*opposite*) brings the Tarascos to the neighborhood church. Italian males often leave religion to their women, but all the Tarascos are devout.

Under a glowering sky, a solitary farmer drives his horse and wagon along a winding road in the dry, desolate hills near Matera. Poo

...s make farming in this region both difficult and unrewarding

5

The South: Impoverished and Primitive

WHILE Italy's southern peasant thinks of Rome and Milan as cloudland utopias fully as remote as America, the man-in-the-street Northerner thinks of all Italy below Rome as a barbarous land in which civilized standards are low and the inhabitants are unkempt primitives.

Both images are exaggerated, but the second less than the first. There are villages in Sicily and Campania where people live with their donkeys in caves. In the city of Naples, scattered underground colonies of humans, living like moles, cough up their tuberculous lungs like the damned in an inner circle of hell. In Apulia, the heel of the Italian boot, there are people who dance the wild *tarantella* to cure themselves of the tarantula spider's bite.

In desolate Calabria some villages have no roads and are approached by way of the stony beds of streams. In Sardinia, bandits gather high on a savage plateau for 10 days each May to make a novena to their patron, St. Francis, asking his protection in their work. In Benevento pre-adolescent children are auctioned for labor on farms. At Palma infant mortality is 10 times that in the North, and if you ask a mother how large her family is she may reply, "We are twenty—ten living and ten dead."

Yet these are the lands the Greeks settled 2,700 years ago and made the center of culture, where the historian Herodotus lived, where the tyrant Dionysius the Elder and the philosopher and mathematician Pythagoras built large followings, and Plato dreamed of establishing his Republic. Here the dramatist Aeschylus died —at Gela—when a tortoise was dropped on his head by an eagle, it is said. These are lands where, in the early 12th Century, Norman tyrants built the most splendid court of the Middle Ages, and where a century later the great Hohenstaufen emperor, Frederick II, made of Palermo a brilliant capital of culture.

HOW did it come about that this onetime center of civilization should be in such despair today? The answer is a complexity of history and geography. But one cause rises above all others: deforestation.

For a case in point, go to the town of Piazza Armerina in the scorched heart of Sicily. You see a limbo landscape of barren gray hills dotted with sulphur mines. Here in 1951 archaeologists uncovered one of the great art treasures of Italy: a mosaic floor extending over a quarter of an acre. The floor, part of the villa of a Fourth Century Roman patrician, depicts hunting and athletic scenes set in verdant woodlands that are alive with game and fish.

When the Greeks first sailed into southern harbors in the Eighth Century B.C., they discovered dripping forests, and these covered the entire southern end of the Italian peninsula. Such a density of oak, ilex, laurel and myrtle still exists on the high Calabrian mountains, so wild and inaccessible that 3,000 years of foresters have not cleared them. But elsewhere the forests have disappeared. To a large extent they were chopped down for quick cash crops and for fuel. *Carbonari* (charcoal burners) and sheep and goats cropping everything green completed the devastation. This happened in Piazza Armerina, and it happened all over the South.

Where the soil is volcanic, as around Naples or on the expansive slopes of Mount Etna in Sicily, a variety of crops flourish. But most of the southern soil is impenetrable clay, and very poor. Sun and rain, each in its season, rarely occur in fruitful combination. During the long rains of winter the clay surfaces become pools of soupy mud, and in the summer the beating sun and hot African winds dry the earth to dust.

Trees, conservers of moisture, would be able to withstand the weather excesses, but the tenderer wheat and corn cannot. Yield is small and crop failures frequent. And with the trees gone the rainfall keeps declining. In Apulia it fell from 32 to 21 inches a year during the 19th Century. Rivers are bone-dry rock beds in summer; in winter they are raging torrents that wash away the soil and loosen mountain slopes, bringing down avalanches to destroy villages.

Deforestation left stagnant pools and swamps for the breeding of the Anopheles mosquito, which spread the South's great scourge, malaria. The disease reached its apex in the late 19th Century when, in areas like Sardinia and Calabria, the entire population was afflicted. The people believed their sickness was caused by *mala aria* (bad air) and they bolted their windows and did not venture out.

Then, as if the earth itself were enraged, the volcanoes of Vesuvius and Etna punished man with eruptions and earthquakes. Promethean Etna has even reached over to the mainland: in 1908 no less than 100,000 persons died in an earthquake that centered in Messina but also traveled across the Strait of Messina to bring great destruction and loss of life in Reggio.

ADD to this the denigrating history of war and plunder—the roll call of invaders after the Greeks includes Normans, Carthaginians, Vandals, Byzantines, Saracens, Spaniards, Garibaldi's red-shirted thousand and the Nazis and Allies of World War II—and one can see how the South slipped into its long coma of despair.

A 16th Century proverb describes the South

as "inhabited by devils," and to this also there is truth. It must be said that the southern peasant is among the most backward in Europe. He is hard-minded, bigoted and superstitious. A small middle class of merchants, professional men and bureaucrats has been lazy, venal and irresponsible, and a majority of the aristocracy consists of absentee landlords living in Palermo, Naples or Rome. Sicily alone has scores of princes, marquises, counts and barons, many of whom drain the wealth from their ancestral lands to support an outdated way of life. The worst devils of all are the racketeering members of the Mafia and Camorra, who in many areas control labor, both agricultural and industrial, as well as markets and ports.

The 19th Century statesman, Count Camillo di Cavour, was the first Italian public figure to proclaim that successful unification required a solution of the southern problem. Above all, the South needed an "iron treatment"—railroad connections with the North—and so the Italian government, carrying out Cavour's program, completed in the early 1900s a railway network from Rome to half a dozen southern cities. An 1,800-mile Apulian aqueduct, bringing water to 300 towns and villages in the southeast, was completed in 1937 after 30 years of labor. Irrigation was introduced and electric-power dams were built. But the improvements were only a beginning, and few lives were changed.

DURING these years, much poverty was alleviated through funds sent home by Italians in the U.S. When emigration fell sharply after the American immigration restriction laws of 1921 and 1924, the South sank still deeper into its malarial torpor, and the North preferred to forget that the other half of the country existed. During the Fascist era the South was a *terra di nessuno*, a no man's land to which Mussolini banished his political enemies, one of whom, the artist-writer Carlo Levi, recorded his experiences in his classic work *Christ Stopped at Eboli*, published in 1946. Not only Levi in Lucania but Ignazio Silone, writing of his native Abruzzi, and Elio Vittorini, writing of Sicily, reawakened

sensitive Italians after World War II to an awareness of southern suffering.

Awareness on a world-wide scale had come during the war itself. Allied soldiers moved through the South from the Sicilian beachheads to Cassino, and at last the misery was exposed to the conscience of the world. Soon United States aid began to flow in a steady stream to Italy, and the Italian government also intensified its interest in the area.

After the war, however, agriculture continued in its backward state, with the *bracciante*, or day laborer, working perhaps only 100 days a year, traveling as many as 25 kilometers to earn a dollar a day. But in 1948 restless bands of *braccianti*, flying red banners, marched on farms and idle lands and threatened to take possession by force. A land reform bill was rushed through Parliament, breaking up many of the large privately owned estates which were not paying their way. Over a 10-year period a total of 1,335,500 acres of land was distributed to farmers throughout the South.

BUT distribution alone was not enough, as was quickly discovered when the difficulty of extracting a living from the land began to overshadow the new-found joy of ownership. Houses with electricity and running water had to be built, as well as stables, poultry runs and silos. Also needed were community centers with those two requirements for an Italian's social life, a church and a movie theater.

In due course these were provided, and efforts were made to educate farmers in deep plowing, drainage and tractor operation. Cooperatives were organized for harvesting, marketing, milk-pasteurizing, wine-pressing, olive oil-milling, tobacco-drying, tomato-canning and cheese-making. The Federation of Italian Agricultural Cooperatives, a quasi-government organization, set up offices, warehouses and sales rooms in 5,000 towns.

In 1950 the government established the *Cassa per il Mezzogiorno*, or Southern Italy Development Fund, to improve agriculture and prepare for industry in the South. The grants, partly from American funds, made possible new roads, hydroelectric dams, irrigation canals, tourist hotels and the kind of public works that nations usually build in their colonies. Courses of rivers were changed, and one entire town was moved down from the Apulian mountains to reclaimed coastal plains. In Lucania a new village, La Martella, was built for the 15,000 cave dwellers of Matera. Experimental cattle farms were set up, and on the bare expanses of former estates, reforestation projects were begun.

In 1957, Parliament ordered the new state-owned industrial groups, the Institute for the Reconstruction of Industry and the National Hydrocarbons Agency, to place 60 per cent of their investments in the South. Work was begun on a new steel center at Taranto, on nuclear power stations at Garigliano and Latina and on petroleum refineries in Sicily's new oil fields at Gela. The Gela oil center, which eventually should employ 4,000 persons, is the most important development in Sicily's recent economic history. Fifty miles from Gela, at Ragusa, America's Gulf Oil Corporation is conducting pumping operations, and at Brindisi on the mainland the private Montecatini company is building a chemical center.

ALL in all, America has poured more than $4.5 billion into Italy, and the World Bank has loaned another $40 million. Much of this has been spent on the South—but simply *on* the South, as one observer has pointed out, and not *in* the South. In short, the millions have flowed first into the arteries of Italy's northern industrial economy, which has supplied both reconstruction materials and know-how to the South. Most of the salaries, for example, have gone to northern engineers and technicians. Private capital, with a few notable exceptions, has stayed out of the South, and even southern investors and banks have preferred to invest in northern corporations. The South's relative share in the national wealth has diminished. In 1952 the per capita income in the South was only 51.5 per cent of that in the North; by 1959 it had dropped to 45.5 per cent. In spite of noble

purpose, of effort and of labor, the North has been growing fatter and the South thinner.

For the poor individual Southerner, the program has produced the *psychology* of change rather than the *environment* of change. The Southerner has his dams and his roads but, except in the case of the fortunate landed minority, they have not yet greatly affected his life. On the other hand, during his public-works employment he found he could earn more in a few weeks' work on a road or school than in months of field labor. It convinced him that there are standards of living different from his own.

HAVING learned the meaning of unemployment, the Southerner is today no longer resigned to the old conditions. He is impatient. Having seen that change is possible, he wants it to come about in his own lifetime. He does not want his children to live without hope, and he is giving Italy only a limited amount of time to prove that democratic institutions must provide work for the people.

His warning is political. During communism's postwar surge in the North, the South was loyal to the Christian Democrats, helping to keep Alcide De Gasperi's party in power. In the general elections of 1953 and 1958, when communism lost in the North or remained static, the party increased its vote in the South by nearly one third. When the Church forbade Catholics to vote for Communists, workmen in Sicily crossed themselves before a statue of the Madonna with one hand and voted Communist with the other.

In the Sardinian town of Alghero, where the state built workers' houses and located 300 families on rehabilitated land, the Communist vote increased as much as 40 per cent, and the town's acting mayor said, "Last winter when we had a most unusual snow in Alghero I think the Communists made the people believe it was the fault of the government."

Beautiful, monolithic Sardinia is the setting for the most impressive single miracle wrought by postwar foreign aid. By treating the island with DDT, American and Italian scientists freed the 1,250,000 Sardinians of the malaria which had afflicted almost every one of them. (Similar programs on the Italian mainland had effects almost as dramatic.) One of the most despairing areas in Sardinia was the province of Nuoro, savagely mountainous heart of the island and lair of bandits.

Here, in the sun-baked town of Oliena, an American visitor attending Sunday Mass found the cathedral packed with richly costumed women—but except for the priest, the acolyte and himself not a single man was present. The men were gathered on the piazza, grimly silent, and one of them explained that the curious situation had existed since an election five months before when the monsignor had threatened excommunication to anyone who did not vote Christian Democrat. The men stopped going to Mass and split their vote between the Communists and the separatist Sardo party. The women voted solidly for the Christian Democrats and won the election for them.

DURING the 1960 centenary week of Garibaldi's Sicilian invasion, a conference on health and living conditions was held in the "typical" western Sicilian town of Palma di Montechiaro, known to the world as the setting for the Prince of Lampedusa's popular current novel *The Leopard*. The meeting was called by Danilo Dolci, a writer and social reformer who, because of his insistence on nonviolence, is being called "Italy's Gandhi."

Investigations had showed that 40 per cent of Palma di Montechiaro's 20,000 citizens were illiterate, that 3,000 of them lived five to a room, and that many rooms were windowless and shared with mules or goats. Eighty per cent of the houses had neither water nor sanitary facilities. Many school children suffered from the eye disease called trachoma, and virtually all had worms. The usual diet consisted of bread, spaghetti, oil and a few vegetables, with meat only two or three times a year.

Dolci, in his shattering book *Report from Palermo*, had also written that almost half of Sicily's population was at least semi-destitute.

He described slums of dark, odorous rooms alive with scorpions, fleas and roaches, where epidemics of typhus, meningitis and tuberculosis were never-ending. In one chapter after another he told of people subsisting on starvation diets. A man's entire life might be controlled by the pervasive, ruthless Mafia, and Dolci counted, in one small area, 520 Mafia murders of which two thirds remain unsolved.

EXPERTS at Dolci's conference concluded that conditions had not improved much in the last 100 years—in fact, they had deteriorated. In an economic and social sense, they said, genuine Italian unification is as remote today as it was when Garibaldi set foot on Sicily. They found that the past decade of relief programs had at best only prevented the rift between North and South from widening as much as it would have if things had been left alone.

Sicily is only one example—though the most dramatic—of Italy's tensions. The two economies, one industrial and the other primitive agrarian, are moving at widely differing speeds. Not until they move together, until the progress and prosperity of the North's modern Italy is extended into the South, will the real frontier of unification be crossed.

The most hopeful portent is that Dolci's conference was held at all. In the eight years that Dolci was in Sicily, he was persecuted by the authorities (both church and state), threatened by the Mafia, frequently arrested and, when his searing book was published, sentenced as a pornographer. The fact that the conference was attended not only by distinguished social scientists and writers but by the archibishop and the president of the region indicates that people with authority may at last be willing to face some truths. At the same time, peoples of the world with more advantages may learn to look with humility on the South. It is still a land that produces the Biblical trinity of life's needs—the grain, the olive and the grape—a land where bread is a holy object which children are taught to kiss before they eat of it and which the family locks up in a cabinet like the Eucharist.

Help for a Tragically Poor Land

A desperate poverty, rare in the western world, submerges Italy's Mezzogiorno, the once-proud southland whose name has an ironically pleasant meaning: "Noonday." Since World War II, the government has contributed huge sums of money and great effort to raise the South out of its misery. Roads and housing, water and electrical systems have been built. Land reform has been introduced. Industry has been brought in, and a campaign of education has been pressed. But the South has sunk so deep that the money and effort barely keep it from sinking deeper.

NEW INDUSTRY overlooks a wheat farm in Casoria, near Naples. The plant, built with help from the government-owned Bank of Naples, produces nylon and Dacron yarn.

NEW HOUSING and six acres have been allotted to former farm hand Giuseppe Quaranta and his family. But Quaranta makes less now than he did working for others.

WEAVING is taught in the government-sponsored school at mountainous San Giovanni. Here an Armenian-born Italian instructor shows how to make an Oriental rug.

THE SOUTH'S HOPE *lies in the people's acquiring new skills that will raise the standard of living. The state is spending millions on training for illiterate farm laborers and members of their families, and some results are already visible*

SEWING occupies farm hands' daughters in the new village of Crocifisso. The domestic science course, run by the state, has enabled these girls to make their own dresses.

WRITING as a teacher dictates, these farmers of Posta Uccello receive the first formal education of their lives. They go to school five times a week, two hours each night.

PRIMITIVE WAYS *persist in agriculture in the South. Using tools that are almost as old as history, men and women stubbornly till the equally stubborn soil to gain the meagerest of livelihoods*

PLOWMAN AT PAESTUM, where roses bloomed in the days of the Caesars, turns his field with an ox-drawn blade. Beside him rise the ruins of a 2,500-year-old Greek temple.

WOMAN WITH A HOE (*opposite*) at Gallo in the Apennine Mountains, 50 miles north of Naples, works methodically to cultivate her husband's farmland by hand.

6

A Shifting Status for Women

TWENTY-ONE centuries ago a large group of ladies marched into the Roman Forum and demanded the revocation of a law prohibiting them from wearing golden bangles and bright gowns. Whereupon the dour senator, Cato the Elder, dared to stand up and warn his fellows, "From the moment [women] become your equals, they will be your masters."

The senator's credo of male superiority has become one of the most persistent myths in Italy's social history. If there is greatness in the Italian woman it is in the unruffled, almost cow-like serenity with which throughout history she has seemed not only to accept but even to abet man's illusion of superiority. The one fact that a wise wife never challenged was that her husband was head of house and home.

By an ancient Roman law that has never been changed, Italian men have *patria potestas*, which assures them full legal control of their children.

Women have little more than residual rights. In most cases, furthermore, the wife does not even supervise the family budget. But she is nonetheless undisputed queen in her own house. By keeping a happy puppet king she becomes the power behind him.

Operating on this principle, Italian women have woven the fabric of national life. In a land where political and economic chaos has been the rule rather than the exception, and where there has been only a small sustaining middle class, the one secular pylon of strength that has held society together has been the family. Today, however, there are signs that family life is not altogether so monolithic as it once was—and this may someday turn out to have alarming repercussions.

THE Italian family has always been virtually inviolable. Divorce is illegal in Italy, and adultery on the husband's part is extremely difficult for the wife to prosecute. While such strictures may seem severe, the Italian woman has cherished them. Rare is the Italian woman who is outwardly perturbed by her husband's infidelity, unless his misconduct is endangering her home. She puts up with it, knowing that by so doing she is preserving the family. Family security makes Italians, even the poorest of them, one of the world's best-adjusted peoples and gives their nation a strength beyond anything that a political system could provide. It may also be one of the reasons why Italians seem to have so little use for psychiatrists.

Italian women are trained to serve men, just as American men are trained to serve women. Not surprisingly, the many marriages between American soldiers and Italian girls, especially lower-class girls, seem—at least at first glance— to have been made in heaven. Since, by the same token, Italian men and American women both expect to be served by the opposite sex, any marriage between them has stood a good chance of being made in hell.

Italy is a land of illusions—all of them belonging to men. Italian women are hard-core realists who not only know but admit that a man who is disenfranchised from his fantasies is a sorry and ineffectual creature. One of the Italian male's illusions is that he is the most comely being on the face of the earth—a magnificent handiwork based on designs by Michelangelo. Because he is jealous of competition, a man will sometimes deliberately marry a girl he believes less beautiful than himself.

Women enjoy seeing their men as strutting cocks of the walk. Stop in a provincial town, perhaps in the South, during the Sunday afternoon *passeggiata*, or community stroll. You will see the normal roles of humanity reversed, as if you were watching not people but a species of bird. Men in all manner of sartorial splendor parade up and down the main street like preening peacocks, while the women, dark and modest as little hens, huddle in clusters to watch the proceedings.

Perhaps the one illusion dearest of all to the Italian male is that he is the world's most irresistible and hot-blooded lover. The shallowness of this was summed up by a Belgian woman who had married an Italian. "They know all about bed," she said, "and nothing about love." Despite the persuasive testimony offered by Italian opera and Neapolitan crooners, there is little romance in Italy. Romance requires sentiment, and sentiment is an Anglo-Saxonism not common in Italy.

THERE are also official hindrances. Two of the sins most stanchly frowned upon by the Catholic Church are communism and sex. In the middle of the 19th Century, Pope Pius IX opposed railroad building because he was afraid tunnels would be a provocation for licentiousness. In spite of official disapproval, however, Italian men make a considerable verbal if not practical obeisance to both communism and dalliance. But it is mostly bluster, since all Italians are by their eternal individualism quite antipathetic to Marxist restrictions, and any extramarital love life is, for the majority of Italian males, largely daydreaming.

Except in Rome and in the prosperous mercantile circles of northern Italy, a young woman is not permitted to go out with a young man. And even among the liberated middle-class families of the North, fathers may go so far as to have their daughters followed by private detectives to insure their prudence. Southern measures are likely to be more brusque, as in the recent case of a Sicilian girl, aged 25, who, feeling herself irreparably damaged by having received a kiss, shot the transgressor when he refused to marry her.

OVER the centuries, strong women have occasionally broken through some of the man-forged shackles. It is significant in such a self-consciously masculine land that one of the patron saints of the country is a woman, Catherine of Siena (the other patron saint is St. Francis of Assisi). Catherine's life proved her worthy of the honor. A practical mystic of the early Renaissance, the formidable Catherine (1347–1380) had her first vision at six, took a vow of chastity at seven and grew into one of the most famed political arbitrators in all history. She traveled to Avignon in 1376 to persuade the exiled Pope Gregory XI, whom she called "my sweet *babbo*," to return to Rome, and later went to Rome herself to bolster the popularity of Gregory's hard-pressed successor, Urban VI.

Like Persephone rising from the underworld, ladies of the ruling classes emerged into the sunlight of equality for a passing moment during the Renaissance. Florence's Lucrezia Tornabuoni (1425–1482), mother of Lorenzo de' Medici, was one of the first women to step out of seclusion into the world of learning and letters. Rich and cultivated Vittoria Colonna of Rome (1492?–1547) was the inspiration of the aging Michelangelo; he was in love with her but never dared to reveal more than spiritual affection for one of the most virtuous women of an unvirtuous era. Vittoria herself wrote creditable love sonnets and religious poems. But the most famous trio of Renaissance belles lived in the North; they were the D'Este sisters of Ferrara, Isabella and Beatrice, and Isabella's sister-in-law, Elisabetta Gonzaga of Mantua.

As Duchess of Urbino, Elisabetta ruled over a dazzlingly intellectual court of poets and musicians. Isabella, who became Marchioness of Mantua, was a scholar and collector known in her time as "the first woman of the world." She also enjoyed jewels and dancing, and had a collection of genuine, live dwarfs, for whom she built a scaled-down apartment in her castle. Isabella's younger sister, Beatrice, became Duchess of Milan at 14 and devoted herself to "all manner of delights." With her husband, Lodovico Il Moro, she made the Sforza castle in Milan the most splendid in Europe before her death at the age of 22.

In Ferrara a pope's daughter, Lucrezia Borgia, who was married to Alfonso d'Este, was the friend of the Italian Renaissance's greatest poet, Lodovico Ariosto. Two generations later, Lucrezia's two granddaughters, Lucrezia and Leonora d'Este, were patrons of another distinguished poet, Torquato Tasso.

The unique sympathy of the people of Ferrara for women leaders was manifested again in our own time when a mild-mannered former high-school language teacher named Luisa Gallotti Baldini became the city's Communist mayor in 1951. But Ferrara's notable women have been exceptions in Italian history. For the most part members of the female sex have stayed in the background, exercising their control over society in an indirect manner.

DURING Italy's Fascist period, a time when women's rights and suffrage spread rapidly in other lands, Mussolini, looking ahead to imperial expansion, maintained policies keeping women in a state of unrelieved maternity. To be sure, even during fascism there were some distinguished individuals among Italian women. One was dark, shy Grazia Deledda, author of strong, stark novels of her native Sardinia and the second Italian to win the Nobel Prize for Literature (1926). Another was the educator, Dr. Maria Montessori, a founder of progressive education for children. For years she traveled widely, making her theories known in Europe, India and the U.S., and when she died at 81 in 1952 the Montessori Method was world famous.

In 1947 the new constitution gave women the vote, and this marked the first big advance in the Italian woman's slow, steady, but largely unorganized struggle against male domination. For the lower classes a strong impetus also came from motion pictures. First, there was the image in American films of the glamorous career girl luxuriating in possessions and handsome admirers. Second, there was the rags-to-riches reputation of the film industry itself. Italy's postwar film renaissance brought to stardom a phenomenal group of new movie beauties, virtually all of whom—like Gina Lollobrigida and Sophia Loren —had to struggle against poverty. In 1950, a report revealed that the ambition of seven out of 10 young Italian girls polled was to become a cinema star, and a whole generation of poor, ambitious mothers were grooming their budding daughters for the Cinderella market.

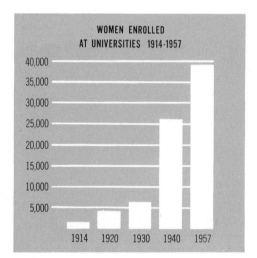

WOMEN ENROLLED AT UNIVERSITIES 1914-1957

40,000
35,000
30,000
25,000
20,000
15,000
10,000
5,000

1914   1920   1930   1940   1957

FEMALE STUDENTS increased greatly in the late 1930s and again after World War II. Women now constitute a third of all university enrollees.

Then came beauty contests, which were copied from America. In a series of competitions that last through the summer, resort towns annually pick a Miss Cinema, Miss Italia, Miss Europa, Miss Mondo, Miss Universo or a Miss Anything Else an ingenious tourist official may dream up. Most of the contestants come from the very poor, and they are sometimes driven to the bathing-suit competitions only by hunger, for being seen in scanty attire in public may involve a considerable loss of family dignity. But the contests are a further indication that the old ways are changing.

Still another new glamor group is composed of fashion models. Compared with the studied and mannered beauty of sophisticated French mannequins, an Italian girl's beauty is natural, with a direct physical vibrancy. When fashion photography began to reveal to the world Italy's long-cloistered race of sultry Venuses, the international reaction of startled pleasure helped bring quick success to the Italian fashion industry. Today the world is becoming increasingly familiar with the names of such noted Italian designers as Simonetta (who is married to the leading male couturier, Fabiani), Princess Irene Galitzine (who can count Mrs. Henry Ford as one of her clients), the Fontana Sisters (who made Margaret Truman Daniel's trousseau) and Biki (who dresses Maria Callas). These women are beginning to be almost as well known as are Coco Chanel in Paris and Pauline Trigère in New York.

Money, of course, has been a powerful motive in women's emancipation. Until the last few years, marriage was almost the only way middle-class Italian women could guarantee that they would always be supported, and even then they often suffered great poverty. As soon as they discovered that they could live by their own labors, the idea of being independent from unrelieved domesticity became more and more attractive, especially in the North. As living costs continued to rise, even husbands became reconciled to the idea of wives having a job and sometimes earning as much as, or even more than, they themselves. For women with children this was, in fact, easier than in America, for Italy still has an ample supply of cheap domestic labor, and in the tightly knit Italian families there is usually a grandmother or an aunt happy to serve as sitter.

Today women are to be found as factory workers, salesgirls, telephonists, radio and television actresses and producers, publishers, and hotel and travel bureau officials. Nearly all state and ministerial jobs are open to them: a woman can be a mayor, senator, deputy or a diplomat.

There are even some women judges, though these are restricted to trying minors, and they are not allowed to hand down verdicts because, according to a male judge, they have such "complex and delicate nervous systems." There are first-rate women physicians and excellent women lawyers in Italy. Libraries, museums and the teaching profession are, naturally, filled with women.

The working girl has had to face a set of uniquely Italian problems. If she walks home alone from work in the evening she is likely to be followed by a skirl of wolf whistles and overtures. She cannot go to a movie unescorted without inviting disaster, and the Sicilian city of Catania has even felt obliged to inaugurate a special bus solely for the use of women who have had reason to dread mixed conveyances.

Outside the ranks of the aristocracy, whose women are generally emancipated whatever part of the country they come from, the most liberated women in Italy are in the North. In

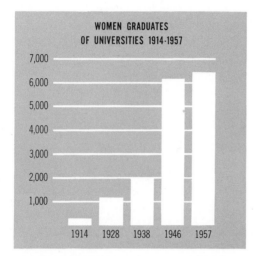

DEGREE HOLDERS have also increased, though not much in recent years. Many women drop out before taking the difficult final examinations.

Milan many women are business managers. One of them, Signora Sylvia Pastore Pisoni, took over her husband's textile-machine agency after his death and subsequently was made a *Cavaliere della Repubblica*, a state honor conferred infrequently on women. Signora Pisoni's career has reflected very closely Italy's changing attitudes on career women. She said, "The beginnings were difficult. Men did business with me by either paying court or treating me badly. I learned the textile process. Slowly I gained a position. In 1951, the year after my husband's death, I went to the opera alone, slightly drunk with champagne. It was against all rules. The following year I ate at the Biffi Scala alone. From that moment I was respected. I have made a position for myself alone. I often travel—Canada, Paris, America—and transact high-level business with men. I have had to give up a number of things. I gave up easy love affairs. Had I done otherwise I would now have many lovers who despised me. Instead I have many friends with whom I am on easy, equal terms."

As you move south from the Po Valley into the isolated country districts, emancipation becomes less and less frequent. Rome is the southernmost point for large-scale female freedom. Sociologists do not expect that women of the lower classes in the South will benefit much from emancipation for another half a century. Nevertheless, the city of Palermo in Sicily now has some 30 lady lawyers, and 90 per cent of the thousands of recent applications for Italy's about-to-be-commissioned corps of 600 policewomen came from southern women.

By far the most controversial of Italy's contemporary career women is the former senator, Angelina Merlin. In 1958, Senator Merlin, a doughty gray-haired lady, won her single-handed 10-year battle with the Italian male to close Italy's 543 state-licensed brothels. The venerable and cherished institutions dated officially from 1888 and unofficially from legendary times. In the 16th Century Pope Sixtus V decided against endorsing a move to abolish prostitution in Rome because driving the ladies of easy virtue and their procurers away would reportedly have cut the city's population in half.

In her campaign Senator Merlin, a former Paduan schoolteacher, cited figures to show that 30 per cent of all Italian women practice prostitution at one time or another. Now that she has won her fight, her parliamentary opponents say that the disenfranchising of 10,000 legal prostitutes has created an uncontrollable army of streetwalkers, and that venereal diseases have more than doubled since the brothels were closed. The avenues of prosperous northern cities are busy with "klaxon girls" operating from Lancias and Alfa-Romeos.

DESPITE all of these changes most Italian women still maintain their traditionally prescribed role of chaste, submissive wife and loving mother. A good many, it would seem, actually love their children *too* much, since one of the great problems of Italy is that virtually every male is a spoiled mama's darling from birth until the age of 30. A large group of young men, products of Mussolini's fertility drives and the victims of postwar unemployment, are known as *vitelloni* or "young calves," a name which writer-director Federico Fellini gave to his excellent film about these undisciplined and irresponsible, *pasta*-stuffed youths.

The only thing that seems to interest the *vitelloni* is quick, easy money to pay for the requisites of a good time—movies, dance halls, jazz records and gasoline for the scooter or automobile. Although a number of them benefit from secondary education, the facilities lag far behind the need, and state high schools are forced to stagger classes and to operate two full working sessions a day.

Still, Italian delinquency is far below that of England and America, no doubt because of such strong family influence as does persist. Many youths attempt to avoid military service. Those who are unable to escape usually learn to their surprise that barracks are a refreshing change after 21 years of rule by mama, and they may emerge from their 18-month soldiering ordeal on their way to becoming useful, mature and adjusted individuals.

There is no doubt that women are shaking the foundations of the traditional Italian way of life. For the moment, the family, solidly upheld both by the Church and, through the Christian Democractic party, by the state, continues to be an anchor. As to how it will all end, not even the women seem to agree. One of the few eminently successful career women, Lawyer Maria Spagnoletti Lanza, who is president of the Italian Union of Women Jurists and the mother of an eight-year-old daughter, said, "I want to see the career of judge and other jobs open for my child so she can have a free choice."

Another woman who has done well, Palma Bucarelli, a Calabrese who is curator of Rome's Gallery of Modern Art, said, "With the Church on the doorstep preventing birth control, it will be a long time before other Italian women have the opportunities I had. Apart from the Church, I blame feminine backwardness in Italy on the women themselves. They are too passive and ready to give way before men."

Other women are also worried. As one has written, "We move slowly, step by step, still deeply conscious of the handicaps that we encounter outside the home in a man's world. The self-assurance of American women is almost inconceivable to us. We view the middle-aged American matron, in whom rests so much social power, as one of the strangest of phenomena." Militant feminists debate among themselves whether anyone can be strictly Catholic and emancipated at the same time. The cautious are afraid that women are imperiling the thing most dear to Italian womanhood and manhood alike: their femininity.

SOME sociologists theorize that the gains on the part of Italian women will act as stabilizing influences on the men and boys. But further upsetting changes may be in the offing. Spurred by their increasing power, a few feminists are now seeking a parliamentary bill guaranteeing women equal rights.

With women voters in Italy outnumbering the men 52 to 48 per cent, the worried males are admitting to themselves that they are in trouble. "Who knows?" moaned one of them. "We may even end up having divorce." Many women, for their part, believe it is now time to take stock. They realize that to destroy Italy's sustaining myth of male superiority would profoundly alter the way of life that has kept the society of Italy on an even keel for centuries.

SPINNING NYLON (*left*) in the Rhodiatoce factory, girls of once backward Casoria work adeptly amid complex machinery.

SELLING SILK in Milan's big Rinascente department store, a salesgirl (*right, facing camera*) remains unflustered by the horde of bargain-seekers around her. Such shops as this, part of a nationwide chain, have wrought many changes for sellers and shoppers alike, providing variety and quality that are difficult to find in the old markets.

EDITOR Franca Matricardi, trained as an engineer, is now administrative head of a big newspaper and magazine chain.

LAWYER Maria Sofia Spagnoletti Lanza heads the Italian Union of Women Jurists. Her husband, a judge, assents to most of her feminist ideas—but objects if she, rather than he, signs their child's report card.

THE EMANCIPATED

*do not yet typify
the womanhood of Italy,
but their gains are
notable, and some have
already attained dominant
positions in the professions*

FASHION DESIGNER Simonetta, who is as chic as the Roman atelier that she heads, is one of a number of talented women who have made Italy's capital a style center rivaling Paris.

MUSEUM DIRECTOR Palma Bucarelli (*left*), here visiting an art show in Paris with France's Minister of Culture, André Malraux (*right center*), is head of Rome's Gallery of Modern Art.

97

APPRECIATION for an attractive passer-by is expressed variously by a number of males on a street in Florence. Girls thus honored generally feign unconcern. This one subsequently married a Venetian count.

Setting off on an upland hike in the mist-clad Dolomite mountains of northern Italy, an area long popular among European mountain

limbers, a group of young Italians starts up from a resort town

7

Playground for a Continent

WHY is the world drawn to Italy? Richard Wagner said the cause was racial "heart hunger," while the French novelist Stendhal, thumping his way through Italian art galleries, said, "The charm of Italy is akin to that of being in love." The poet Robert Browning wrote:

> *Oh, woman-country, wooed not wed,*
> *Loved all the more by earth's male lands,*
> *Laid to their hearts instead!*

The German, the Frenchman and the Englishman, all courting the mistress of the world! The mystical power of Italy began simmering the day the first handsome blond barbarians marched down from the Alps to overwhelm—and to be beguiled by—the dark-eyed pastoral people of the lands to the south. Take your pick of explanations of the chemical affinity of opposites: the compulsive attraction of fair for dark, cold for warm, male for female.

Because writers and artists, the peripatetic

prophets of every land, have loved this country the most, Italy has had the best publicity in the world. One of its first press agents was Christina of Sweden, who, abdicating her throne in 1654, went to Rome, wangled a sinecure from a seemingly defenseless pope and gathered about her a court of scientists and poets. After her death the beneficiaries of her largesse met in a Roman garden to memorialize her by founding an academy of learned men. They called it Arcadia, after a district of the Greek peninsula inhabited by contented shepherds, and the name eventually came to stand for devoted, intense striving after intellectual and artistic good taste both on the part of foreign visitors to Italy and among Italian artists and writers themselves.

An anachronism in the politically turbulent Italy of its day, the romantic Arcadian movement caught on with esthetic foreigners, whose muses were undisturbed by politics and who brought with them an appropriate ingenuousness. John Milton came to visit with Galileo, and Edward Gibbon, while reflecting among the ruins, was inspired to write his epic *Decline and Fall of the Roman Empire.*

Not surprisingly, visitors in the classical 18th Century cared little for the Renaissance and even less for the Middle Ages. The American painter Benjamin West went straight to the Vatican's Apollo Belvedere, then considered the most perfect work of art in Italy, and cried, "How like a Mohawk warrior!" The poet Goethe, making a peninsula tour, visited only classic monuments. In Assisi he bypassed Giotto to visit the Temple of Minerva. Simultaneously Thomas Jefferson was making sketches of classic-revival buildings, which he would later consult while designing the University of Virginia.

WHEN the defeat of Napoleon in 1815 reopened the roads of Europe, a far bigger Arcadian invasion began. One of the first arrivals was the young American writer, Washington Irving, who, because his ship had been waylaid by cutlassed pirates on the Mediterranean, expected to be attacked by bandits on the mainland. Instead he dined with cardinals. Next came

the romantic British triumvirate, Byron, Shelley and Keats; the latter two died there and were buried in Rome's Protestant cemetery. From Denmark came sculptor Bertel Thorwaldsen and fairy-tale writer Hans Christian Andersen; from Norway, playwright Henrik Ibsen, to hike all over the Papal States. From France came the writers Emile Zola and Théophile Gautier, and the feminist authoress George Sand, who walked across Italy dressed in men's clothes, carrying a knapsack packed with cigars.

As the century progressed, from Germany came the poet Heinrich Heine and the philosopher Friedrich Nietzsche, and from Hungary the composer Franz Liszt, who became an *abbé* in the Catholic Church in Rome. From Russia came novelists Ivan Turgenev, Nikolai Gogol (who called Italy his "true homeland" and wrote most of *Dead Souls* there) and Feodor Dostoevsky (who wrote *The Idiot* in Florence). From England came an entirely new conglomeration of writers: Samuel Taylor Coleridge, William Makepeace Thackeray, George Eliot and the manic-depressive master of esthetics John Ruskin. Above all there were those most celebrated of all 19th Century expatriates, Robert and Elizabeth Barrett Browning.

THE liveliest Arcadians were the Americans. Painters by the score covered acres of canvas with the ruins of Paestum, shepherdesses with tambourines and Appian tombs in a romantic style known as "drawing-room art." For a writer not to know Italy was a calamity, and so literary tourists were legion. James Fenimore Cooper rode across the Campagna on a white charger, and James Russell Lowell jogged across Sicily on a mule. All over the place were Herman Melville, historian Francis Parkman, suffragist Julia Ward Howe and Harriet Beecher Stowe (who commemorated her trip by writing a novel called *Agnes of Sorrento*).

Abraham Lincoln appointed author William Dean Howells to the U.S. consulship at Venice, where his major duty was looking after traveling American ladies. Howells' closest friends were the two great incompatibles of American letters, Mark Twain and Henry James. Both arrived in the 1860s. Twain, the original man from Missouri, jokingly said "Renaissance" was a man's name, called Italy "that vast museum of magnificence and misery," and described Venice as looking "so like an overflowed Arkansas town . . . that I could not get rid of the impression that there was nothing the matter here but a spring freshet." James, the refined New Englander, bolted through Rome in a fever of excitement and exclaimed, "At last—for the first time —I live!"

There were also some oddballs. One of them, Connecticut spiritualist D. D. Home, carried Mrs. Browning away with his seances, in one of which he was reported to have suspended the Countess Orsini's piano in mid-air while the countess continued playing it.

IT was the great era of Victorian exuberance, stirred by what the English librettist W. S. Gilbert described as "Fascination frantic/ In a ruin that's romantic."

Rome was the most beautiful city on earth. You sat in the Forum to reflect on the glories of the ancient days, you excursioned to Tivoli to inspect Cardinal Ippolito d'Este's water works and you visited the Colosseum by moonlight. So hallowed a tradition was the third that Fanny Appleton, wife of the poet Henry Wadsworth Longfellow, refused to look at the ancient amphitheater by daylight. Most of the novels that the Arcadians wrote dealt with Americans in Rome. In Nathaniel Hawthorne's *The Marble Faun*, the puritan heroine Hilda, shattered by witnessing the murder of a monk, escapes into a Catholic confessional. The heroine of Henry James' *Daisy Miller* makes a moonlight foray into the Colosseum and later dies of malarial fever and a broken heart. ·

The dream of Arcadia reached a fulfillment in the early 20th Century when some highly gifted visitors made their stay permanent. Writers Norman Douglas and Max Beerbohm from England, philosopher George Santayana and critic Bernard Berenson from the U.S.—all made Italy their home. Berenson in particular became

the quintessence of the true Arcadian, raising art scholarship to a new plane of exactitude.

So many intellectual, self-appointed publicity agents breaking into print naturally aroused widespread interest. When non-Arcadian Europeans and Americans with the needed funds and leisure decided around the turn of the century to see for themselves, a new age of Italian tourism was inaugurated. Young English and German aristocrats took a six months' culture-soaked "grand tour" that centered in Florence. Russians preferred the Byzantine opulence of Venice, but almost everyone took in Rome and the Neapolitan coast. For a while Ferrara, one of the most shining jewels of the Renaissance, was popular among the visitors. Then rumor spread among travelers that it was unhealthy, and although the unhygienic conditions were corrected, the city dropped from favor.

Except for the interruptions of wars, tourism in Italy has continued to grow. Even World War II brought special benefits to the country: the invasion first by the Germans and then by the Allies introduced a whole new generation of young people to an amiable land and people. After the war many of the soldiers on both sides returned, to make Italy more than ever a place of relaxation from the restraints and rigors of northern life. Today Germans are the largest group of visitors; after them are the Austrians, Swiss, French and British. Americans rank only sixth, though they stay longer and spend more.

MOST of the visitors come chiefly for sightseeing, for which Italy, in both the multiplicity of its arts and the variety of its bright landscapes, is the richest land on earth. Rome has continued to be the most popular city. Admirers of classical antiquity, of course, help make it so, as do religious pilgrims. As the capital of world Catholicism, Rome draws throngs of nuns and monks, who bustle up and down the streets with the exuberance of a Tintoretto painting of paradise. In addition, thousands of pious lay people come hoping for a papal audience or simply to visit St. Peter's and the nearby monuments of their faith. Indeed, it often seems as if the visitors are what make Rome the Holy City. Though the capital has several hundred churches, the Romans themselves are not overwhelmingly religious. A 19th Century pope, asked to restore Holy Week rituals which had been allowed to lapse, replied, "Why not? It will amuse the English."

Florence, a city whose wealth of architectural and artistic masterpieces make it a museum in itself, is second to Rome as a magnet for tourists. The Tuscans who inhabit it are among the most genial folk in Italy, and on Florence's streets one may recognize a face he has seen on a Masaccio fresco or in a painting by Botticelli. Aside from elderly English ladies, who always travel in pairs like Italian policemen, Florence is popular with a new species of visitor, the American academic on a Fulbright scholarship. In the past 10 years about 1,200 government-endowed young students have gone to Italy for a year or more.

OPALESCENT Venice, which looks almost more like the paintings it has inspired than any real city could, is third in popularity after Rome and Florence. The dreaminess of its character does not extend to its worldly citizens, who for three frantically busy summer months seem to turn into just so many itching palms to bedevil the 700,000-odd tourists. But in an earlier day, when this was no problem, John Ruskin found it "the paradise of cities." Byron and Shelley and William Wordsworth all praised it with poesy. A cluster of sun-drenched islands abounding in slinking cats, arrogant pigeons and decorative towers (several of them leaning), Venice is Italy's last refuge from the internal-combustion engine. The automobiles and roaring scooters which have turned the streets of Rome into speedways and Florence's Piazza della Signoria into a thundering racing rotunda are mercifully banned from Venice.

After the great cities, the most popular region for tourists in Italy is Mount Vesuvius' domain, the stretch of mountainous coastline from teeming Naples to Salerno. Traversed by a vertiginous road spiraling above cobalt bays,

its lemon-scented villages clinging to the cliffs like swallows' nests, it has what is perhaps the world's greatest concentration of natural beauty. Norman Douglas called it "Siren Land" and based a book on the premise that Homer's singing Harpies had abandoned Greece and migrated there. The legend has come to curious reality in recent years for native fishermen, who in their gill nets occasionally catch human sirens wearing diving masks and big rubber flippers. Nineteen centuries ago the Emperor Tiberius, ruling Rome from Capri, gave the *divina costiera* (divine coast) its reputation for unbridled wickedness, a distinction that was perpetuated by Norman Douglas in his elegantly scandalous novel *South Wind* in 1917.

SERIOUS sightseers are drawn to the ruins of Pompeii and to Paestum's temples to the south. For writers and artists the area has had a special attraction. Wagner found inspiration for *Parsifal* and D. H. Lawrence for *Lady Chatterley's Lover* in the elevated solitude of Ravello. H. G. Wells and Edith and Osbert Sitwell worked in Amalfi, the seaside village where Henrik Ibsen wrote *A Doll's House*. The Russian writer Maxim Gorky lived on Capri, where his occasional guest, Vladimir Ilich Lenin, fished and played chess.

Below the "divine coast" on the traditional tourist map there is only Sicily. Goethe, whose voyage from Naples to Palermo took more than four seasick days and nights, correctly observed, "Italy without Sicily casts an imperfect image on the mind. The key is here." Sightseers go to Palermo for the Byzantine mosaics, Moorish palaces and baroque churches; pleasure-seekers concentrate on the Greek towns of Taormina and Syracuse at the eastern end of the island. Taormina, suspended between the sea and volcanic Mt. Etna, has been called the most beautiful place on earth—and this may be true. One of its most noted visitors was the Rev. John Henry Newman, the Anglican clergyman who subsequently became a cardinal in the Roman Catholic Church. Looking down from the hilltop ruins of Taormina's Greek theater in

1833, Newman later recalled, "I felt for the first time I should be a better and more religious man if I lived there."

Italy has two rivieras, one on the Mediterranean in the west and the other on the Adriatic in the east. The Ligurian coast in the northwest follows the arc of the Gulf of Genoa from San Remo, near the French frontier, to La Spezia, east of Genoa. During the summer the area is populated by wealthy industrialists from Turin, Milan and Genoa. The tycoons own houses in Portofino, Rapallo and Santa Margherita, and moor their boats in the nearby harbors. The coastal region, cut off by mountains from the northern winds, has a mild climate in the winter, when it is popular with retired Englishmen escaping the harsh weather at home.

The 80-mile stretch of dazzling white sand along the Adriatic in the east is Italy's most spectacular single beach. Here the present-day Germanic influx is most apparent; each summer 200,000 Germans, Austrians and Swiss gather for a holiday romp reminiscent of a portrayal of the gods on Mount Olympus. Italians call it the Third Gothic Invasion, the first being the Fifth Century conquest by barbarians and the second the Nazi occupation of World War II. Here, too, flocks of *pappagalli* or "parrots" (the name given to eager local males) roam the streets seeking out sunburned northern Loreleis to console. Since many "parrots" wear wedding rings, enduring loves are seldom born, though the girls from Zurich and Munich usu-

ally consider their holidays memorable enough.

The east coast's tourist center is Rimini, a town long governed by the Communists. It has a boardwalk of shops, beauty parlors, bars and nightclubs which advertise in three languages, "Special prices for tourists." An astonished Englishman who had just been required to pay an exorbitant price for a cup of coffee once said, "Special prices indeed. These Reds are bloody free enterprisers!"

To the north are the diaphanously misty lakes, Como, Garda and Maggiore, the last of which extends up into Switzerland. Frequented by the rich of Milan and northern European countries, the lakes were once sleepy, jasmine-scented refuges. Now they roar with the raucous motors of speedboats and reek from the exhausts of open-vented sports cars.

Italy's newest tourist loadstone is the island of Sardinia. When the Roman, Quintus, had to go there 2,000 years ago, his brother Cicero wrote, "Take care, my brother, of your health." The dismal trinity of malaria, poverty and banditry kept almost all visitors away. D. H. Lawrence, making a querulous journey there in the winter of 1921, suffered such arctic discomforts that the Sardinians seemed to him to resemble Eskimos. Largely from vexation he wrote *Sea and Sardinia*, one of the great travel classics of modern times.

Years later, in the early 1950s, after malaria was eliminated from the island, large numbers of Germans, Scandinavians and Englishmen,

TEN FAMOUS ITALIAN WINES

Chianti	Red or white, tart, very popular	Tuscany
Barolo	Red, dry, full-bodied	Piedmont
Valpolicella	Red, dry, delicate	Veneto
Soave	White, dry, pleasant	Veneto
Orvieto	White, dry or slightly sweet	Umbria
Est-Est-Est	Golden, moderately sweet Muscatel	Latium
Verdicchio	White or pink, dry, light	Marches
Lacryma Christi	White or red, moderately dry, aromatic	Campania
Frascati	White, dry, fruity	Latium
Marsala	White, dry or sweet	Sicily

BEST-KNOWN WINES made in Italy are shown in the chart at left. Italians drink an average of 34 gallons of wine each year. The North produces more good varieties than the South does, but one of the most noted is Marsala, favorite drink of England's Lord Nelson. Italy is one of the world's paramount wine exporters.

crowded off Italy's mainland in their pursuit of a cheap vacation, began going to Sardinia—perhaps remembering Lawrence's book. They found a passionately wild landscape and a curiously gentle people who, like lonely islanders everywhere, were warmly hospitable.

Sardinia's capital, Cagliari, is a shimmering white city hanging from a hillside, seemingly about to plunge into its bay. On the northern end of the island, surrounded by olive groves, is Sassari, a relaxed center of learning and culture, and a half hour's train ride away is Alghero, a sea-washed, wind-swept fishing community of Spanish character. In the spring the limestone town, covered by a thick orchid-colored flower called *bella di giorno*, is a pink-carpeted bastion of gold rising from the indigo waters like a holy city.

OF the small islands, one of the most popular is Elba. Napoleon's temporary place of exile (he was there for nine months in 1814), it is a sun-bathed resort off the coast of Tuscany. Some of its remote, pastel-tinted villages never knew an automobile until five years ago. Before World War II Elba was a tranquil summer retreat for the noble and rich families of Florence and Rome. Then, during the war, the Germans occupied it—and liked it. After the war they returned in multitudes. An Elban, paraphrasing the rise of the West German economy, said, "They came first on foot with rucksacks, then with Volkswagens. Now they come in Mercedes-Benzes." Germans fill up the new luxury hotels and several large camping grounds. Their cars—and those of rich young Italians—speed over the new cliff roads, and at night everyone dances to orchestras playing calypsos and tangos.

Italy below Naples was once a tourist's no man's land, an area of bad roads and few habitable inns. Norman Douglas, exploring it in 1911, found a startlingly beautiful landscape, ports with an oriental splendor, Romanesque cathedrals and medieval castles. In the heel of the boot he met up with a fair-skinned blond people who seemed to him to be more Greek than Latin. Though he reported his trip in *Old Calabria*, few people felt moved to follow him.

It was many years before the man came along who finally did open the Italian South to visitors. He was Count Gaetano Marzotto, an energetic woolen textiles tycoon who today is one of Italy's richest men. In the South on business one night in 1949, Marzotto found himself unable to locate a decent hotel and had to sleep in his car. The government in Rome was apathetic to his plea for publicly constructed hotels, and so he decided to build a few himself. He called each one a "Jolly," the Italian word for the joker in a deck of cards—a lucky thing to find. Marzotto now has 19 Jollys south of Naples, plus 11 in Sicily and six in Sardinia. They are clean and comfortable, and the prices of the rooms are scaled for the Italian middle class.

For the epicurean, Italy is even more gratifying than France, for every town has its own gastronomic specialties and wines. There are a few gourmet shrines: Rimini's Giardino Restaurant, which serves only fish; Rome's La Fontanella, which specializes in wild game, and Bologna's La Cesarina for *pasta* and sausages. The Bolognese consider their town the gastronomic capital of Italy, though a steady diet of *tagliatelle*, *tortellini* and *mortadella* sausages is likely to be, like the people who eat them, somewhat heavy.

AS one observer has said, pleasure in Italy serves two masters, the foreigner and the Italian. The gulf between the two, furthermore, is almost unbridgeable. One reason is temperament. Visitors from northern Europe, while they are entranced by the peninsula's beauties, are likely to be exasperated by the Italian's casual unconcern for detail, and they are frequently shocked by the pagan practicality of his Catholicism. On the other hand Italians, who look upon drunkenness as a debasement, fail completely to comprehend the excesses of some of the visitors. An American tourist who is kicking over the traces of a strict upbringing is scornfully called an *americano italianizzato*, an American "trying to act like an Italian."

An even greater barrier between the two kinds

of leisure is financial. Most Italians simply cannot afford the pleasures that occupy the tourists. Only on beaches and in Milan and Rome do natives (well-to-do ones, at that) and tourists ever play together. These cities contain an affluent minority who ski at St.-Moritz and fly to New York for balls and receptions (their pleasure trips frequently coinciding with business). The wealthy Milanese pay up to $1,600 for a season's box at La Scala opera house, and listen to American jazz in a cellar night club next to the cardinal's residence. In Rome a popular bistro is La Grotta Del Piccione, where Mussolini's son Romano plays a cool jazz piano. Rome's night clubs, taking a third of their revenue from foreigners, are run with Renaissance ruthlessness and have friendly girls with cash registers beating where their hearts should be. As with café society in any land, neither the pleasures nor the seekers represent Italy.

DIVERSIONS are not so expensive for humbler Italians. According to a national poll, the most popular pleasure is also the cheapest: it is "conversation with friends." Italians engage eternally in what strikes foreigners as dangerously heated argument but is actually friendly discourse. An Italian prefers to be heard rather than to hear, and the most successful conversationalist is the man with the loudest voice.

Equally inexpensive is the national finger game of *morra*. Nothing, seemingly, could be less exciting than counting an opponent's dancing fingers. Yet the antagonists gesticulate so violently that they seem to be possessed with diabolical passions, and their frenzies sometimes fire them to disputes which have been known to end in murder.

Italians are card addicts. All men play *tre sette* ("three sevens"), *scopone* and *briscola*, and women of the upper classes are bridge and canasta enthusiasts. Every Sunday morning, and frequently during a midweek twilight, working men play *bocce*—bowling with wooden balls—on a vacant lot next to a church or café, or even in the village piazza.

A large percentage of Italian men are devoted hunters, and the government licenses five million of them a year. The pursuit of food is a major motive for this, and centuries of gunning have left little game to be hunted on the entire peninsula. There are still wild boar in Sardinia, ducks in the Po marshes and a few bear and rabbits in the mountains, but small birds are now the most popular quarry. Unfortunately, Italian hunters have a compulsion for shooting and netting songbirds during the autumn and spring migrations between Africa and northern Europe. The toll of thrushes, warblers, finches and swallows, all of which Italians are fond of eating with corn-meal porridge or in sandwiches, is probably 100 million a year. Indeed, the practice is straining Italy's diplomatic relations with West Germany, the Netherlands and other bird-fancying countries, whose songbird populations are being cut drastically by the semiannual massacre.

For many Italians the most colorful and animated entertainments are the various saints' festivals. And for tourists these are the sideshows of Italy. The traditionally undernourished Sardinians follow an image of their gluttony-paunched patron, St. Efisio, across the island, feasting and drinking all the way. In Marino, an old Roman fortress town, the new wine is dedicated to the Virgin each October with a community bacchanalia during which wine actually flows from public fountains. Northern towns revive medieval hostilities with brilliantly costumed mock wars. In Gubbio the townspeople shoot it out with crossbows. In Arezzo they joust on horses, in Venice from boats and in Pisa on narrow bridges. Inhabitants of Marostica, near Vicenza, play a human chess game with marvelously costumed chessmen moving on a giant board drawn on the town square.

IN Florence the butchers from one side of the Arno and the butchers from the other side dress like Medicean princes for a game of wild soccer, no holds barred, while cannon shots boom the time signals. Most explosive of all festivals is Siena's *palio*, a boisterous horse race staged around the old town square by jockeys who have previously ridden their mounts into the church to have them blessed.

Because travel is expensive, few Italians are sightseers. If they journey at all it is as pilgrims to Rome or to the holy shrines of Loreto and Syracuse, and they usually carry their own supply of bread, wine and roast meats with them. The working classes on vacation go either to the mountains or to the seashore. Few working-class Italians are fond of swimming, though in the summer's heat some may venture into the water. Germans and Scandinavians who bathe in February are considered hopelessly mad. But the newly popular sports of skin-diving and spear-fishing are drawing more and more youths of the leisure classes into the sea. Northern Italians have become converts to sun-bathing. In the hot South, however, the peasants remain convinced that removing their clothes in any season is an invitation to illness.

AS Italians rise in the economic scale, their amusements become more varied. Most young Italians who can afford it are ski enthusiasts. From northern cities they go to the Alps or the Dolomites. Romans ski in the Abruzzi mountains east of the capital, Sicilians on the slopes of Mount Etna. Horsemanship, tennis and fencing, too expensive for most Italians, are diversions for patricians, and water polo and sculling occupy the young elegants of Florence, Rome, Naples and Palermo.

Almost all Italians are devoted followers of spectator sports. Bicycle racing has long flourished, and its champions have become better known than prime ministers or movie stars. A star cyclist, earning as much as $80,000 a year, may be watched by 12 million people during the course of a single race. Auto racing had almost as big a following until a series of road fatalities in the mid-1950s led to government restraints; the famous Mille Miglia race, which had thrilled Italians for years, was discontinued in 1958, though public demand brought it back after one year. Sicily's round-the-island Targa Florio, dating from 1906, still continues. In Monza and Milan there are motorcycle races.

Most popular of the spectator sports is *calcio* (soccer), about which an Italian feels as deeply as an American does about baseball. Most of the large cities have teams; Rome and Milan each have two. Players are imported from Sweden, Denmark, Argentina and England and earn as much as $60,000 a year, and a game in Rome's Olympic Stadium can easily draw 100,000 spectators. In the South, rioting fans have on occasion been seriously wounded by broken bottles and even by gunfire.

Directly related to soccer is Italy's most universal diversion: betting. Each week Italians wager more than two billion lire—three million dollars—and half of this goes into the government-sponsored Totocalcio, a weekly soccer pool. Half of the pool goes to the winners and half is divided between the C.O.N.I. (Italian National Olympic Committee) and the Italian government. There are also betting pools for horse and greyhound racing, plus a national lottery called Il Lotto, based on the venerable game of lotto (which was invented in Genoa more than 300 years ago). For a poor people, the rags-to-riches myth of gambling has a hypnotic fascination, and the pool and lottery chances, usually costing 100 lire each, are sold like postage stamps.

SOMETIMES tourists buy the bright tickets of chance, but they seldom win. No one is surprised. Perhaps the world of the Italian and the world of the stranger did overlap to some extent in the days of the great Arcadians. But that era finally came to an end in the 1950s, with the deaths of Norman Douglas on Capri, George Santayana in Rome, Max Beerbohm in Rapallo and Bernard Berenson in Florence. In the Olympic year of 1960 more than 18 million visitors came to Italy. Unless they ventured outside the splendor of St. Peter's, the smart hotels, the baited bistros and the fashionable beaches, they could not come to know the Italian people. If, however, they had taken to the humbler roads that lead into the hills and small villages, they would have discovered the human riches which Italy has so overflowingly to give.

On Rome's fashionable, tree-lined Via Veneto, Romans and tourists alike take their coffee and apéritifs at Doney's sidewalk tables

A Gusto for Good Living

Italians are convinced that it is good to be alive, and they spend considerable time and energy proving themselves right. With gusto, they sail on warm seas and chill lakes, bowl in the nearest back yard, race about sun-baked soccer fields or argue among themselves at a sidewalk café. But nothing reflects their enjoyment more than their cookery, which is as diverse as the nation's regions, as imaginative as the Italian character. Whether the cook presides in a swank hotel or an ancient farmhouse, the meal is likely to be superb. For, to an Italian, to eat is to live.

As twilight gathers in Venice, delectable dishes await a diner at the Hotel Royal Danieli. The table offers polenta (left), liver, seafood

110

soup, grilled scampi, the crablike granseola (right) and a spun-sugar dessert. In the background is the Church of San Giorgio Maggiore

THE SEA, *never far away,*
is a source of work, of pleasure
—and of food in a land
short of beef. The sea brings
fortune, says an Italian proverb,
and for ages mariners, shipbuilders
and fishermen have proved it

BATHER AT RIMINI, a bearded Turin businessman, has spent his holidays thus for 40 years. Taken there first by his father, he "wouldn't think of going elsewhere."

BOATERS AT CAPRI explore the Blue Grotto (*opposite*), a cave in the Bay of Naples which was famous even in the days when the Emperor Tiberius lived on the island.

DINERS AT NAPLES choose a fish dinner with the help of Signor Attolini, exuberant proprietor of the Ristorante d'Angelo, which commands a fine view of the huge bay.

BIG-CITY BATHERS from northern centers like Milan delight in basking on a boat on mountain-ringed Lake Como.

FROLICSOME FRIAR of a Carmelite monastery near Rome (*opposite*) has fun spinning a disk resembling a big yo-yo.

In an engraving by famed illustrator Paul Gustave Doré of a scene from the Inferno, Dante (right) and his guide, the Latin poet Vergil,

witness the torture of simonists—those who traffic in sacred objects

The Turbulent Awakening

IN the past decade and a half, Italy has witnessed a modest rebirth in the field of literature. New writers have come to the fore, and today the rest of the world is intently observing the country's literary output. The new activity is only an echo, however, of an incomparable earlier day when Italian letters were the glory of western civilization.

Italy's great literary Renaissance began in the 14th Century, when three exceptional Florentines fell devastatingly in love with beautiful women at first sight. These women inspired three triumphs of the spirit: Dante Alighieri's *Divine Comedy*, Francesco Petrarch's Italian love lyrics and Giovanni Boccaccio's *Decameron*.

Of the three Florentines, only Dante was actually born in Florence, and all were wanderers frequently absent from the city of their fathers. It was a turbulent time both politically and theologically. From teaching posts in Rome, Paris and Naples in the previous century the Dominican friar Thomas Aquinas had reconciled

Aristotelian logic and metaphysics with Christian dogma. In short, he had enthroned Reason alongside Faith as a guide to the knowledge of God. Soon the new doctrine was in the thick of politics. Secular rationalism became the philosophy of the insurgent Ghibellines, while the politically entrenched Guelphs, regarding learning with suspicion, rejected the new rationalism and adhered to the simpler, heart-impulsive doctrines of the Franciscans. The new spirit had little immediate popular influence. For most people life was severe, relieved only by an occasional religious festival or the coming of a band of minstrels. But educated men were shaken out of their comforting certainty.

THERE had been foreshadowings of an awakening. In the 13th Century the troubadours of Provence and the minnesingers of Germany had sent their lyrics and come in person to savor the brief so-called "Sicilian Renaissance" of Frederick II, a poet himself. But 13th Century poets were too often formalists who wrote ponderous Latin verses in dead forms. To sing, purposefully and in the vernacular of the people, the praises of beautiful women and of idealized, personally felt love was still a revolutionary concept. The three Florentines who sang with such exuberance were all vitally involved with secular living.

The first, Dante, was still a man of the Middle Ages. He was born in 1265 of a poor family of the minor nobility. He met his immortal love, Beatrice Portinari, at a May Day feast when both were nine years old. Because he did not meet her again until both were 18, after which she married someone else, Dante's passion is surely one of the most idealized in all history. Dante himself later married another woman and had several children, but he glorified his spiritualized feelings for Beatrice in verse and prose long after she had passed away.

He also busied himself with politics. As a leader of the deposed "White" party in Florence, he became an exile to Arezzo, Bologna and Padua. After writing a provocative Latin treatise in which he advocated a world state under the Holy Roman Emperors, he was exiled permanently by Florence. Homeless and increasingly bitter, he wandered to Gubbio, Lucca and Verona, all the while writing his long poem *Commedia* (known as *The Divine Comedy*) as a sort of apologia for his stormy life. In his concept, Inferno was the suffering and despair of his exile, Purgatory was his cleansing by faith, study and writing, and Paradise his redemption of hope through divine revelation and through his unselfish love for Beatrice.

Grim, austere, his wits sharpened by adversity, Dante took revenge on his enemies by relegating them in the *Commedia* to the deepest pits of hell. He never forgot an injury, and few of his adversaries escaped the acid of his pen. He poured all that life had taught him into his great poem, and only three years after it was finished he died.

He had begun it in the conventional Latin, but to reach a broader audience he turned from the dry style of theologians' language to the living Tuscan vernacular. His poem established the "vulgar tongue" as a beautiful language of letters and the Tuscan dialect as the cultural tongue of all Italians.

IN 1302, the same year in which Florence's aristocratic "Black" party exiled Dante, a "White" Florentine lawyer known as Ser (Master) Petracco was forced to flee to Arezzo. There after two years was born to him a son, Francesco Petrarca (as he later wrote his name). The family moved to Pisa and, when that city became unsafe, to Avignon in France, where the recent establishing of the papal court had created a demand for lawyers. Growing up in France, Francesco was sent to Bologna to study law. Instead he read the classics—Vergil, Cicero and Seneca—and after three years returned to Provence, the land of the troubadours.

It was in an Avignon church on Good Friday, 1327, that Petrarch (as he is known to English-speaking peoples) first saw the woman who was to make him the most famous poet of his time. Laura is thought to have been the wife of Count Hugues de Sade, and in any event she kept the swooning Petrarch at a distance, encouraging him only with her denial. While she bore her husband 12 children Petrarch wrote 207 love poems, gathering them in a *Canzoniere*, or songbook. Back in Italy the verses were found to be the loveliest music of words ever heard, making even Dante seem sometimes stilted and crude. Italian speech, with its singing vowels and its uncompetitive consonants, had found its place as a supremely lyrical language.

BY replacing artificial allegories with real-life entanglements, Petrarch helped make love poems a literary form and taught Italians the art of courtly love. Because of his explorations of the human ego and his concern for classical intellectual values, he has been called the first modern man and the first humanist. Although in his search for happiness he was occasionally troubled by the double truths of theology and humanism, and although he was deeply critical of the Church of his time, he united pious devotion with an enthusiasm for pagan civilization. The politics which consumed Dante only slightly concerned him. An ordained priest who in a series of amours fathered at least two children, he could hardly have known that he was also fathering the Renaissance.

Petrarch was called "venerable master" by Giovanni Boccaccio. The illegitimate son of a Florentine merchant, Boccaccio was born in Paris, the result of a business trip by his father, who brought him back to an unhappy childhood with a stepmother in Tuscany. At the age of 10 he was sent to Naples to learn finance and trade; instead he read Ovid, the Roman poet of love. On Holy Saturday, 1331, just four years after Petrarch encountered Laura, Boccaccio discovered *his* lady love, also married, and also at Mass. She was blonde Maria d'Aquino, illegitimate daughter of Naples' King Robert the Wise. He thought her superbly lovely, he called her Fiammetta (Little Flame) and he longed to be burned. He must have read early Dante and Petrarch, for his poems, like theirs, were filled with yearning and passion, and he ended one of them with a phrase later echoed in Verdi's opera *Rigoletto:* "*Giovane donna è mobile*" ("Woman is fickle").

Perhaps to impress her with sheer volume, Boccaccio wrote Fiammetta an epic poem of nearly 10,000 lines. Unlike Beatrice and Laura, Fiammetta succumbed. After a year of expensive assignations, the flames of passion died down, and early in 1341 Boccaccio abandoned Naples for Florence, where he pursued women personally and in poetry and prose.

During the Black Plague, which from 1348 to 1365 killed half of Italy (including Fiammetta), he wrote the 100 prose tales which constitute his *Decameron*. Surrounded by the dying, the life-loving Boccaccio celebrated living with narratives drawn from the classics, from Oriental tales and from folklore. He made ribald fun of chastity, the confessional, hypocritical priests, monks, nuns and even saints. The world saw itself in the mirror and laughed at what it saw. Translated into every European language, this masterpiece of the early Renaissance has held its popularity through the centuries, while Dante and Petrarch have passed into that twilight of being praised universally but read only for patriotic or scholarly reasons. From the first years of the many-faceted Renaissance, Dante addresses humanity's soul, Petrarch speaks to humanity's intellect and Boccaccio to the pagan joy of life.

THE reawakening was called *la Rinascita* (the rebirth). People were becoming interested in science and no longer considered it irreconcilable with religion. Frederick II had had his own astrologers (about the closest thing to genuine scientists in the Italy of his time); now even popes and bishops consulted their astrologers before making any important decisions. Florence, second only to Venice in riches, was dominated during most of the 15th Century by history's greatest patrons of art and learning, the Medici family. The banker Cosimo de' Medici, caring as much for literature and art as for wealth and power, turned his city into the cultural capital of Europe. He imported precious cargoes of manuscripts from Alexandria and

Greece, employed 45 copyists and made free translations available to teachers and students. Under Cosimo's influence, Aristotle's reign was halted in Florence and Plato was enthroned. The humanists treated Christianity as a proper myth for popular belief, to be taken seriously by emancipated minds more for reasons of social propriety than for spiritual discipline. They set Italians thinking about philosophy instead of religion, about man instead of God, and they revealed to an amazed but eager people the wealth of classical thought and art. Even those who could not read saw beauty and pagan joy in the great pageants which the Medici and other leading families presented in their cities.

Cosimo's grandson, known as Lorenzo the Magnificent, wrote vernacular love lyrics in the style of Petrarch. No one embodied Renaissance morals and manners so completely as this man —ruling a state wisely, managing a family fortune, jousting in tournaments, sponsoring artists and authors, singing bawdy songs with the peasants, composing hymns and dallying with mistresses. His imitators spread the Renaissance to Rome, Milan, Venice and Naples; and popes, importing poets and artists to the Eternal City from all over Italy, made their courts the most brilliant in the world.

FOR a time the top literary court was at Ferrara, where the three D'Este brothers, Leonello, Borso and Ercole I, were among the most refined and enlightened rulers of their time. Ercole, father of those belles of the Renaissance, Isabella and Beatrice d'Este, translated into the vernacular the Latin plays of Plautus and Terence and had them performed.

The most distinguished of the D'Estes' many pensioners was the High Renaissance's greatest poet, Lodovico Ariosto. His swashbuckling epic of Charlemagne's knights, *Orlando Furioso*, upon which he worked a dozen years, is Italy's most beloved poetic masterpiece after *The Divine Comedy*. It is loved by Italians much as Shakespeare's plays are revered in England. During the reign of Ercole's great grandson, Alfonso II, the court was host to the poet Torquato

Tasso, whose great work is *Jerusalem Delivered*.

Renaissance amorality and artistic perception reached their peak with Pietro Aretino, friend of the painters Titian and Tintoretto and the most scurrilous and successful writer of his day. Employed early in his career as a kind of court jester to Pope Leo X, Aretino moved around Italy making enemies until 1527, when he took up residence in the last city left to him, Venice. He wrote plays, "conversations" between prostitutes and lewd sonnets, as well as a series of religious works including *The Life of the Virgin Mary*.

IT is important to observe the profligacy to which "enlightenment" had led the age in order to understand the intellectual revolt of two Florentine reformers, Girolamo Savonarola and Niccolò Machiavelli.

Born in Ferrara, Savonarola was a pious and bookish youth who at 23 ran away to a Dominican monastery in Bologna. Small-framed, swarthy and Satan-ridden, he became prior of the Monastery of San Marco in Florence, where his apocalyptic sermons, according to a contemporary, were "so full of terrors and alarms, cries and lamentation, that everyone went about the city bewildered, speechless, and, as it were, half dead." Lorenzo de' Medici tried to appease Savonarola with gifts, but these he scorned. Lorenzo died in 1492, leaving a weak son. This cleared the way for Savonarola to become the strongest power in Florence. He organized a moral police force of children to collect "vanities," a word he applied to "immoral" pictures and books like the *Decameron*, precious manuscripts, playing cards, musical instruments and immodest dress (which the children tore from women). All of these were burned in a gigantic bonfire on the Piazza della Signoria.

By 1498, the long-suffering Florentines—as well as Pope Alexander VI—had had enough, and on May 23 of that year the unfrocked and barefoot Savonarola and two accompanying friars were hanged from a gibbet and their bodies burned in the same piazza. A medieval figure surviving into the Renaissance, Savonarola was ultimately destroyed by the age he condemned.

The moral corrosion was observed also by Niccolò Machiavelli, who became a Florentine functionary the year of Savonarola's execution. Machiavelli spent his early life as an envoy to various European courts, but in 1512 he became a political exile when a citizens' militia he had formed in Florence was defeated by the Medici. He spent his last impoverished 15 years writing books analyzing the stormy political situation about him. Of these, by far the most famous is *The Prince*.

His philosophy was almost exclusively political. To him, politics was a high art: creating, holding and strengthening a state should be man's loftiest ideal. He attempted to find out why states rose and fell and how their inevitable decay could be deferred as long as possible. War was good because it strengthened society; when a state lost its will to war, it was finished.

Unlike Savonarola, Machiavelli blamed the Church for Italy's moral and political decay. Four years before Martin Luther nailed his theses to the Wittenberg church door, Machiavelli wrote, "If the rulers of Christendom had kept their religion in the form in which its Founder established it, Christian republics would be much more united and prosperous."

THOUGH both Savonarola and Machiavelli suffered personal defeat, both helped end an era. The Counter Reformation returned authority to the Church and to foreign rulers. The 200-year interlude between Petrarch's birth and Machiavelli's death was over. Descending night ended Italy's glorious springtime day.

The country's vitality was quelled, its spiritual wings clipped. Many gifted Italians emigrated to foreign lands, spreading the Renaissance throughout Europe. Italian culture and language spanned the world, while at home only music remained free enough to flourish.

In the 18th Century in Venice, Carlo Goldoni briefly revived classic comedy, writing in a formalized French style. In the political-minded 19th Century three authors rose above intellectual insularity and provincial patriotism. There was Giacomo Leopardi, fervent atheist poet, and Alessandro Manzoni, devoutly Catholic author of the influential novel, *I Promessi Sposi*. In their contrasting attitudes toward the world and eternity, the Neapolitan Leopardi and the Milanese Manzoni represented the spiritual polarity of Italy. The third figure, Poet Giosuè Carducci, was able to combine Italy's pagan heritage with its new national aspirations.

THE greatest of Italian novelists after Manzoni was the Sicilian Giovanni Verga (1840–1922), who introduced *verismo*, or naturalism. His little novels of peasants and fishermen include *Cavalleria Rusticana* (which inspired the opera by Mascagni). Another great regionalist was Grazia Deledda, Sardinian poet-novelist whose peasant novels, *Elias Portolu* and *The Mother*, led to her being awarded the Nobel Prize in 1926. The Sicilian Luigi Pirandello was one of the most distinguished playwrights of the period between the two great wars.

The two decades of fascism were difficult times for writers, but nonetheless some superior works were produced. In voluntary exile Ignazio Silone wrote the novel *Bread and Wine* and G. A. Borgese wrote the noted historical analysis *Goliath: the March of Fascism*. During his involuntary stay in Lucania, Carlo Levi gathered material for his penetrating *Christ Stopped at Eboli*, which shook the conscience of the world.

With the collapse of fascism, Italian literature came into the rebirth which has attracted so much recent attention. The most popular writer has been Alberto Moravia, some of whose best works are short stories. According to Moravia, the short story has been a popular Italian medium since Boccaccio for the very reason that the novel has not. Italians, he says, dislike looking into the mirror for very long. Unable to bear introspection, they want to move away quickly.

Although Italy today publishes some 14,000 titles a year, few sell well enough to assure their authors an adequate income. Writers support themselves by taking jobs in journalism or by writing for the movies, television and radio. More than 90 per cent of all Italian books are published in the North. The great books which Italy has been giving the world since Dante are still the concern only of an educated and prosperous minority.

The country's North-South schism is nowhere so apparent as in the realm of intellectual institutions. Most of Italy's museums and research institutes are in Milan, Rome, Turin and Florence. Thirty out of 41 universities and institutes of higher learning and 15 out of 18 important academies of music and art are in the North. Many of these institutions are of top caliber. The most noted universities are those of Rome and Bologna; and Bologna is Europe's oldest.

But there is no escaping the fact that Italy is one of the most illiterate nations in Europe. A large percentage of Italian children do not enter school at all. In some regions of the South, illiteracy is as high as 53 per cent, and in 1948, 65 per cent of Calabria's townships were without schools. One fifth of all Italians over six years of age are only semi-literate, and almost two thirds read nothing but an occasional newspaper. The vast majority of Italy's newspapers are in the North, and two southern regions publish no daily papers at all. Yet many prominent editors and writers have been Southerners.

ONE of these was Italy's only intellectual titan of modern times, the humanist philosopher Benedetto Croce. For more than half a century the lord protector, if not dictator, of Italian culture, Croce was Italy's most eminent thinker since the 17th Century scientist Galileo.

Croce was born in 1866 in a small village in the province of Aquila, the son of a wealthy landowner. When he was 17 his father, mother and sister were killed in an earthquake, but young Benedetto miraculously escaped with serious injuries after being buried several hours. The rest of his youth was a difficult recovery from pain and sorrow.

He was fortunate in having an independent income which permitted a leisurely life of travel and study. He is well known for his critiques of Marx and Hegel, but his major work was the several-volume *Philosophy of the Spirit*.

Croce's political career began in 1910, when he was elected a senator. At the end of World War I, faithful to his Machiavellian ideals of nationalism, he opposed the League of Nations as a sorry remnant of a Masonic and 18th Century mentality, which he had always scorned. At first he looked on fascism as a reform movement and lent his vast prestige to Mussolini. But two years after the Duce's "march on Rome" he broke with the dictator. Later Mussolini was reported as saying, "There is one man in all Italy whom I fear—Croce—and I fear him because I do not understand him."

CROCE made his last public stand against Mussolini in 1929, when from the Senate floor he vigorously attacked the signing of the Lateran Pact with the Vatican. After that he was expelled from one academy and society after another, and his home was almost wrecked by Fascist thugs. Only a grudging respect for world public opinion restrained Mussolini from openly harming the venerated philosopher.

Meanwhile all Italian intellectuals were reading Croce's voluminous work and his magazine *La Critica*. He became the strongest anti-Fascist voice in Italy, and thousands of Fascist-schooled young men switched to Croce liberalism in their university years.

Though he was Italy's most distinguished anti-Communist, Croce had a huge influence on the intellectual development of Italian Communist leaders. He helped in the re-establishment of Italian democracy after World War II, then retired from active politics in 1947. In his last years he considered himself an arbitrator between what he called Italy's "two churches," the Catholic and the Communist, while they fought for the allegiance of his countrymen.

Croce's humanism was concerned entirely with the heart of man, and his passions were a flowering of the richest and most endearing qualities of a great-hearted people. Before his death in 1952 he said, "I am often asked if I believe that the future belongs to freedom. My answer is that freedom has no need of the future—it already possesses eternity."

In the glitter of lights reflected in a box-side mirror, an opera's cast responds to acclaim on the stage of Trieste's Teatro Verdi

Pleasures of Mind and Heart

In the realm of the mind, the Italian is dominated by emotion rather than logic: he delights in living life rather than in philosophizing about its meaning, and he takes his intellectual pleasures accordingly. He approaches grand opera (*above*) not as a cultural exercise but as a sensual experience. When he reads, he prefers literature that reflects the times and troubles of ordinary human beings. Serious books have a limited audience because education in general is limited. Even total literacy, however, would be unlikely to affect the ordinary Italian's earthy outlook on life.

WRITERS *of today delve below the surface of modern life, and some focus on social protest. Even poets who are immersed in the classics take sides politically*

ALBERTO MORAVIA, a master of the novel and the short story, probes the intricacies of human relationships in a sensual style that blends realism and a sense of drama.

SALVATORE QUASIMODO (*left*), a poet who abandoned communism to enjoy literary freedom, won a 1959 Nobel Prize for his lyrical verse dealing with human suffering.

CARLO LEVI was trained as a physician and prefers to think of himself as a painter, and his work ranks with the best in Italy today. But he won fame with his book *Christ* *Stopped at Eboli*, which described the abject poverty of a small village in the southern region of Lucania. He continues to write for Italian newspapers and periodicals.

125

EDUCATION *remains one of the nation's gravest problems.*
Although Italy founded its first institution of higher learning in the 11th
Century, public schooling lags. Millions of citizens still cannot read

SIMPLE TASKS, the girls sewing, the boys writing, are performed in a school in Matera, a southern town.

LEARNED TALK absorbs a group of scholars (*right*) at the University of Bologna, now nine centuries old.

The great builder, Pier Luigi Nervi, is haloed by the huge dome of his Olympic Sports Palace in Rome. A master of reinforced concrete,

Nervi upholds a tradition set by Italy's Renaissance architects

9

Glorious Era in Art and Music

WHEN a foreigner ponders Italy's contribution to the world, he is likely to think first of its Renaissance painting and operatic music. And these are fields in which the country has never been surpassed. For almost two centuries, the land was a workshop for an outstanding collection of painters and sculptors. When their era was over, Italy's creative energies were diverted to musical composition that was no less glorious in its beauty and significance.

Italy's age of artistic leadership began in the 13th Century, when a simple Tuscan shepherd boy looked at the natural world with wondering eyes as if he were seeing it each day for the first time. Because he painted exactly what he saw, Giotto di Bondone (1266?–1337) became the father of western painting and, like his poet friend Petrarch, one of the founders of the Italian Renaissance.

There had been great painting before on the Italian peninsula. One can see it in the lusty Hellenic frescoes in Etruscan burial tombs and in the languidly sensuous nudes on the excavated walls of Pompeii. But the early Christian Church found the brush too flexible for its doctrines. Like manuscript illuminations, Church pictorial decorations were done in a rigid Byzantine style, first in shining mosaics at cathedrals in Palermo, Ravenna and Venice and then in glittering painted copies of mosaics on the altars and walls of lesser churches. Most artists were anonymous journeymen, generally monks, who used bright red, blue and gold hues to mass-produce Christs that looked like awesome oriental kings, Holy Infants wizened as old men, and almond-eyed, heart-faced Madonnas with scarcely an emotion in their countenances.

BEFORE Giotto, there had been Cimabue (1240-1302), a Florentine artist whose Madonnas, while still stiff, had a hint of gentle humanity. According to popular legend, Cimabue found the young shepherd Giotto drawing on a slate and took him to Florence. By drawing and painting with a new kind of naturalness, Giotto launched a revolution. He replaced the stiff and gloomy images of tradition with live people and some elements of real landscapes, reproducing them on a plane surface with soft luminous coloring and with some feel for three-dimensional forms. Portraying men and women in the movement of life, he brought human narrative to art.

During the eventful century which ensued, Italian artists followed his example and his inspiration. Though working in the new humanist style, the Church-sponsored artists painted mostly religious subjects. The man who took up where Giotto left off was youthful Tommaso Guidi di San Giovanni, nicknamed "Masaccio" or "Big Thomas." To a Giottoesque style he brought light and shadows and the perspective of a single beholder. But Masaccio's painting life was short. He died in 1428 at the age of 27.

Some of the most distinguished names in art history became his posthumous pupils. One of the first was pious Fra Giovanni, whom his fellow friars came to call Fra Angelico, "angelic brother." The mild friar happily painted holy pictures in blazing gold, vermilion, scarlet, blue and green for churches and for monastery cells. For him, painting was a joyous religious exercise like prayer, and his intention was to inspire piety. His faces, almost too beautiful and gentle to be human, seemed like flowers in paradise.

A more worldly friar was Filippo Lippi. According to the Renaissance art historian Giorgio Vasari, "Filippo is said to have been so amorous that when he saw a woman who pleased him he would have given all his possessions to have her, and if he could not succeed in this he quieted the flame of his love by painting her portrait." One of his models, a nun in a Prato convent, eloped with him, and while serving as a model for some of his many Virgins she bore him a son, later famed as the painter Filippino Lippi.

Florence also had sculptors. Twenty-five-year-old Lorenzo Ghiberti in 1401 won the commission for the portal of the city's baptistery and spent almost 50 years sculpting scenes from the Bible on two pairs of doors. Ghiberti's studio became a school of art nurturing a dozen geniuses, one of whom, Donatello, soon excelled the master. With his helmeted David, Donatello reintroduced the nude statue to art. No one had sculpted unclad free-standing figures since the days of the Romans.

In 1469, 20-year-old Lorenzo de' Medici, the most notable member of an amazingly influential family, came to power in Florence. Of him Vasari wrote: "All those who studied in the gardens of the Medici . . . became excellent artists. This can only be ascribed to the exquisite judgment of this great patron . . . who would not merely distinguish men of genius, but had the will and power to reward them."

ONE of Lorenzo's early pensioners was Andrea del Verrocchio, or "True Eye." This painter turned sculptor was a prototype of the legendary Renaissance man who could do all things in the arts: he could paint, sculpt, set jewels and even compose music. Verrocchio's studio was a workshop of the arts to which Leonardo da Vinci, among others, came to study.

But painting, not sculpture, was becoming the favorite art in Florence and other centers, and two important new painters were Domenico Ghirlandaio and Sandro Botticelli. The son of a goldsmith, Ghirlandaio was an amiable character who, because he could refuse no requests for paintings, sometimes painted too quickly. Botticelli, however, surpassed Ghirlandaio. This darling of the Medici was a young sensualist who turned more and more to pagan subjects. His wistfully voluptuous canvases, *The Birth of Venus* and *Primavera*, represented a loosening of the Church's control over subject matter.

Pope Sixtus IV may have realized what was going on, for in 1481 he beckoned Botticelli to Rome to paint some religious frescoes. When the artist came back to Florence, Savonarola's sermons had darkened the spirit of the town and the Church's power had revived. Botticelli was deeply impressed. His Venuses became Madonnas, and with the decline of the Medici he sank into obscure poverty and painted no more.

Savonarola's sobering mood fell on painters like a pall. Lorenzo di Credi spent half his life painting devout Madonnas. Fra Bartolommeo carried all of his nude paintings to Savonarola's bonfire in Florence's Piazza della Signoria, and thereafter painted Madonnas and saints. Andrea del Sarto, however, painting Virgins with his beautiful wife as model, still managed to display his warm enthusiasm for the female form.

Although there was turbulence in the "city of flowers," Florence's artistic influence was nonetheless spreading to other northern centers. Piero della Francesca painted with a noble purity in Urbino and Arezzo. Luca Signorelli turned out paintings of nudes all over central Italy, his best in Orvieto. In Padua, Andrea Mantegna, in love with antiquity, painted saints in Roman dress, and on a ceiling in Parma, Correggio had the apostles sitting on clouds like Olympian gods.

THE Renaissance's three greatest artists— Leonardo, Raphael and Michelangelo—were men who belonged to no one city. Of the three, Leonardo da Vinci was the most enigmatic. The painter of *Mona Lisa* and *The Last Supper*, he was famous also as a draftsman, sculptor, musician, engineer, inventor and mathematician. A crudely cynical man without moral conviction, he said, "*Io servo chi mi paga*" ("I serve whoever pays me"). To prove it, he hired out to the celebrated military leader, Cesare Borgia, as an engineer when Borgia was preparing to subjugate the artist's own Florence.

Leonardo had been for a time in the Milan court of Lodovico Sforza, where his duties included decorating stables and making girdles for Lodovico's bride, Beatrice d'Este. In 1516, after the Sforza dukes surrendered to the French monarch Francis I, Leonardo went to France to become a court painter and engineer. There he died three years later, already a legendary figure in both science and art. Throughout his life he had filled notebooks with remarkable drawings of anatomy dissections, ideas for new inventions and facial caricatures in which he explored human ugliness.

THE happiest genius of the Renaissance was Raffaello Sanzio. The mighty papal patron of art, Julius II, by inviting most of the great artists to the Vatican, had moved the Renaissance capital from Florence to Rome, and in 1508 Raphael was summoned to paint the Pope's apartments. So pleased was Julius with Raphael's results that he dismissed his other artists, ordered their paintings whitewashed and asked the new man to paint them over. The Vatican frescoes, which Raphael took three years to complete, constitute a majestic panoramic allegory of Renaissance civilization in which classic culture is artistically united with Christianity.

Raphael's favorite theme was the Madonna; he painted 50 versions, which today are spread over the western world from Washington's National Gallery to Leningrad's Hermitage. When he died at 37 in 1520, all of Rome's artists accompanied his body to its tomb in the Pantheon.

The Pope's real favorite, however, was the third of the titans, the *terribilità* Michelangelo Buonarroti, and Julius called him frequently to Rome. Michelangelo's first fame had come with the *Pietà* which he sculpted for St. Peter's basilica. In Florence he toiled two and one half years on a heroic male nude statue called by the people *Il Gigante*, which was actually his David.

When Julius called him back to Rome in 1508 to paint the ceiling of the Vatican's Sistine Chapel (named for Pope Sixtus IV), Michelangelo protested that he was a sculptor, and recommended Raphael instead. But Julius insisted, and the artist, lying on his back on a scaffold, spent four and a half years covering the ceiling with athletic nudes that suggest sculpture. Michelangelo had no interest in landscapes or in anything else but the human form. In a hundred-odd panels he told the Biblical story of man's origin, starting with the creation of Adam by a majestic Zeus-like God, and all Italy agreed that a sculptor had accomplished the greatest painting achievement in history.

J ULIUS died four months after the Sistine ceiling was finished, and Michelangelo returned to Florence. There the Medicean Pope Clement VII, bearing with patient fortitude Michelangelo's changing moods, kept the artist busy with building and sculpting commissions, mostly on the Medici family's chapel and tombs. Then politics interfered with art. Florence had been a republic for two years when in 1529 a German-Spanish army arrived to restore the Medici family to power. Michelangelo, though a long-time Medici artist, turned into an anti-Medici engineer and builder of walls and forts. When Florence fell and the republican leaders were sentenced to death, Michelangelo scurried back to Rome.

The golden age, he found, was over. He was a ghost from another era. Pope Paul put him in command of architecture and art at the Vatican, and set him to work painting *The Last Judgment* over the Sistine Chapel altar. With it Michelangelo became part of the religious renewal that is called the Counter Reformation. Three popes died, but the old artist lived on. Pius IV refused to accept his resignation, and so Michelangelo continued as architect of the new St. Peter's until his death in 1564 at 89. His passing marked the wane of the Renaissance, but his position as the greatest artist who ever lived has been acclaimed by the western world to this day.

The Renaissance sun finally set in the east, in Venice. Ignited late, Venice burst into a blaze of oriental color and opulence in the late 15th and early 16th Centuries. The prime innovator was no Venetian but a Sicilian vagabond named Antonello da Messina. The only artist of rank to come from southern Italy, Antonello brought to the Adriatic city a radical technique of oil painting he had learned from Flemish painters.

The Venetians were too infatuated with color to match the drawing skill of the Florentines. There were nevertheless seven masters of the Venetian school: Gentile Bellini and his brother, Giovanni; their follower, Carpaccio; the elegant Giorgione; the formidable Titian, who was still painting his riotous mountains of pink flesh when he died at 99; the irreligious Tintoretto, who produced dramatic religious canvases; and Paolo Veronese, who painted Christ and the saints as if they were a conclave of Venetian millionaires. Compared with Giotto's pure and affectionate prelude, it was a cynical postlude.

Though the end was at hand, however, Italian ebullience was not to be repressed. With the authority of both church and state blighting the development of literature and art, the tremendous creative energies of the Italian people were concentrated on a more abstract and less censurable realm: music.

F OR no other art do the Italians have more natural talent than they have for dramatic vocal music. The most extroverted and demonstrative people of the Mediterranean, they have since Dante and Petrarch spoken a language that is the most melodious in the world. Furthermore, the Italians seem peculiarly blessed with throats which naturally emit sweet, free-flowing sounds. Perhaps this is because they have been essentially a pastoral people free from many of the tensions of urban life—even when living in cities.

Italians are a singing people. St. Augustine admitted to having been moved by vocal music, and the early Christian Church, while attempting to suppress secular sensuous music, retained that which was considered to be spiritually elevating. Psalm singing adopted from the Hebrews led to antiphonal singing, which was introduced to the West by St. Ambrose in the Fourth Century. In a quiet monastery in the Po marshes in the 11th Century, a monk by the name of Guido d'Arezzo invented a system of clear, precise musical notation, setting the basis for the development of music as a recorded art. The first known composer of madrigals was a friend of Dante named Pietro Casella.

Since the Catholic liturgy, above all the Mass itself, is filled with emotional drama, it was natural that the first great Italian master of music

SOME NOTED ITALIAN OPERA SINGERS		
Adelina Patti	1843-1919	Soprano
Antonio Scotti	1866-1936	Baritone
Enrico Caruso	1873-1921	Tenor
Tito Schipa	1889-	Tenor
Beniamino Gigli	1890-1957	Tenor
Ezio Pinza	1895-1957	Basso
Renata Tebaldi	1922-	Soprano
Cesare Siepi	1923-	Basso

OPERATIC STARS over the last century are shown above. Besides the all-time favorites, the list includes recent singers whose place in opera history seems assured.

should have been a composer of Masses. His name was Giovanni Pierluigi, and he is known as Palestrina from the town where he was born in 1525. He wrote a constant stream of sublime Masses and motets which even the Jesuit-hating Richard Wagner three centuries later found "a spiritual revelation." Palestrina's successors called for new instruments, and from a workshop in Brescia came the viola, the oldest member of today's violin family.

The first opera, a tragedy called *Dafne* by Ottavio Rinuccini, which was set to music by Jacopo Peri, was performed in Florence about 1594. *Dafne* was little more than a pastoral play, but it and Peri's *Euridice* (1600) made possible the work of the genius who created modern musical drama: Claudio Monteverdi. A few years later, in his *Orfeo* (1607), Monteverdi gave the musical content of song a new importance, and moved the dramatic action by means of an orchestra much larger than had been used before.

From Monteverdi down through Mozart in the 18th Century Italy was the center of music, the absolute monarch of the art. Other countries had individual composers like Bach and Purcell, Haydn and Gluck. Some were individually greater than any contemporary Italians, but each was more a personal phenomenon than an expression of national glory. Italy had an astonishing roll of prolific composers like Alessandro and Domenico Scarlatti and Antonio Vivaldi. The German Georg Friedrich Handel, writing for the London stage, helped make Italian opera the rage of Europe. The Austrian Wolfgang Amadeus Mozart wrote Italian-style operas to Italian librettos. (Not robust enough for Italian taste, however, Mozart has never been truly popular in Italy.)

By the beginning of the 19th Century, Germany had taken undisputed leadership in instrumental music and France in opera. But two Italian composers returned a large part of the glory to Italy. The first was Gioacchino Rossini, whose comic *Barber of Seville* in 1816 electrified Europe and made its composer more famous than Beethoven. The second was the Sicilian Vincenzo Bellini, composer of *Norma* and, before his death at 33, three more operas whose unending streams of soaring melodies both encompassed and freed the human voice.

The operatic stage was ready for Giuseppe Verdi. With his knowledge of stagecraft and his profound insight into human behavior, this 19th Century giant filled the theaters of the West with dramatic passion and vocal virtuosity. In a dazzling array of popular operas, he made music an eloquent language speaking to —and for—all mankind. A later composer, Giacomo Puccini, set a smaller stage but created melodies that were even more contagious.

For Italians, opera is a national sport which they attend to hear their favorite stars manipulate the high passages. They treat their singers as Americans treat baseball players, hailing them with shouts if they succeed and shrill whistles if they fail. Allegiances to prima donnas and opera houses are as heated as American allegiances to the Dodgers or the Yankees. Italy's opera houses are state-subsidized, and while their presentations are often inferior to those in Vienna, Munich or New York, Milan's La Scala can offer performances unsurpassed anywhere. Italy has four world-renowned contemporary composers—G. Francesco Malipiero, Ildebrando Pizzetti, Luigi Dallapiccola and Goffredo Petrassi—but the Italian public has little interest in new music and these men are little thought of at home.

Italy has produced no great painters since the 16th Century, but in the early 20th both Amedeo Modigliani and Giorgio de Chirico were acknowledged masters of the international "School of Paris" style. Since World War II Italian painters have turned wholeheartedly to abstractions. There are many names, but the best known in America is Afro Basaldella, who signs his flashy canvases with his first name, and Giuseppe Santomaso, who evokes the calm moods of his native Venice. Among the recent sculptors is Mirko Basaldella, brother of Afro, who models metal abstractions and teaches at Harvard University. Two other modern sculptors, Giacomo Manzù and Marino Marini, are also keeping Italy's reputation high in that field.

WHAT is there left, what is the living heritage in this country which has produced such exalted literature, such great painting and sculpture, and so much glorious melody?

In our time, the Italian genius is again expressing itself in architecture. Italians have always been builders. From the Alpine chalets in the northern mountains to the palaces of Palermo, the buildings of Italy are more varied perhaps than those of any other country in the world. Some of the greatest artists of the Renaissance were the builders. Filippo Brunelleschi made architectural history with his monumental dome for Florence's cathedral. Donato Bramante of Urbino, Michelangelo of Florence and Giovanni Lorenzo Bernini of Naples rebuilt Rome for the popes. The 18th Century classic revival based on the work of Andrea Palladio spread throughout Europe and England to the United States, where it influenced design in colonial New England and in Washington, D.C.

The close of World War II left much of Italy a rubble heap, and the construction which began almost at once provided infinite opportunities for a new generation of builders. The greatest is Pier Luigi Nervi, technically not an architect but a structural engineer whose modern pantheons, beautifully honeycombed with concrete ribs, serve as airplane hangars, factories, exhibition halls and sports arenas.

Then there is the cinema, which Italians for a brief time in the postwar years raised to a high art. Here also the war contributed, for imaginative directors like Roberto Rossellini, Luigi Zampa and Vittorio De Sica, having neither studios nor funds, were challenged to use all the artistic creativeness at their command. The result was a series of poignant classics. But these *neo realismo* films, praised throughout the world, were never popular in Italy, and Italy's motion picture industry turned to making the mediocre Hollywood type of glamor film which the Italian public prefers.

Something, it is altogether too clear, has happened to the countrymen of Dante and Giotto, Michelangelo and Verdi. If there have been oppressive influences, one would be the Church, struggling to control philosophy, science and the arts, and containing its people in a kind of social stagnation. Another was fascism—20 years of methodical stupefaction which severed the Italian people from their noble past and from the intellectual changes of the 20th Century.

PERHAPS it was inevitable that a people living in poverty and ignorance should suffer a debasement of spirit. To some critics, Italian taste seems to be on a dismal course: the land which made the western world its spiritual province is adopting with gusto the most base components of western materialism.

Even so, there is reason to hope. The nation of Leonardo and Galileo has always produced superbly practical visionaries. In the new 20th Century era in which art and science are again united, men like Nervi may be pointing the way to greater heights.

Molding the Image of Mankind

The urge to create beauty has impelled Italy's sculptors for more than 2,000 years and her painters for hundreds. The sculptors and painters are still at work, but Italian artistry now expresses itself in many media. The imagination of Italian architects impresses colleagues in every country. Sketches by Italian industrial designers change the shape of American cars. Rome's dressmakers rival those of Paris. From hair style to shoe style, Italy has remolded the look of western man and woman. This is in keeping with a great tradition, for the Italians, whose art embellishes the following pages, have long influenced the concept of beauty.

135

TRIUMPH of the new in sculpture, this large bronze door of the Baptistery in Florence is the work of Ghiberti, who was born in 1378. The detail below depicts Joseph and his brethren, along with two scenes from the life of Benjamin.

THE GREAT ERA *for Italian art began in the 13th Century with Giotto's painting. Soon sculptors too were developing fresh and humanistic styles*

BREAK WITH THE PAST, Giotto's *Life of Christ* shattered the centuries-old precedent that Jesus and his family had to be depicted as fleshless, wholly spiritual beings.

Giotto, a Tuscan born about 1266, blended reality and holiness in his work, of which *The Nativity* (*above*) best retains its hues. The paintings adorn a chapel at Padua.

MASTERPIECES *of art have been limned and shaped by Italian brush and chisel for ages. The greatest were born in the years of the Renaissance, but the tradition survives to this day*

LIGHT AND SHADOW frame the enigmatic smile of Leonardo da Vinci's *Mona Lisa*. The world's most famous portrait, it hangs in the Louvre in Paris.

CLASSICISM AND PAGANISM blend in Botticelli's *Birth of Venus* (*in detail, opposite*). The painting portrays the goddess of love rising up out of the sea.

PIETY AND MAJESTY are united in a Madonna and Child by Michelangelo (*right*). The statue has stood in a small church in Bruges, Belgium, for 450 years.

WARM COLOR expresses the sensuality of Titian's *Danaë and the Rain of Gold*, done in 1545. The great Venetian painter turned to more religious themes in later years.

DRAMATIC LIGHTING distinguishes Tintoretto's titanic depiction of the Three Kings before the Infant Jesus (1583–87). In his day such treatment of light was unique.

DEEP DEVOTION dominates Raphael's Sistine Madonna (*opposite*), in which St. Sixtus, St. Barbara and cherubs adore the Virgin and Child. It was painted around 1515.

ABSTRACT MURALIST Afro Basaldella typifies the bold, imaginative trend in modern Italian painting. The artist, a native of Udine now working in Rome, once taught at Mills College in California, where he maintained this huge studio filled with abstractionist sketches. On the easel is part of a mural for the UNESCO building in Paris.

ABSTRACT SCULPTOR, Afro's brother Mirko is head of Harvard University's Design Workshop. Here he dabs acid to turn a metal Virgin green.

IN THE SLUMS of an Italian city, a woman and a little girl wanly observe the activity about them. Poor living conditions are a major problem before the government.

10

Hopeful Road for an Enduring People

YOU are back in Naples. It is a warm afternoon and the city seems as carefree and happy as usual. Barefooted fishermen with leathery faces are beaching their bright boats, chanting as they work. A band of smallish boys gathers to feast on the tiny fish discarded from the nets. As quickly as the men toss the fish aside, the children pounce on the wriggling fingerlings and throw them onto a fire, roasting them alive.

Darkness falls and the gay clamor calms.

Naples at night is another place. The city is a cobblestone jungle of soft voices and softly menacing shadows. Prowling the night streets are a special kind of children, more terrible in their way than Savonarola's 15th Century infant crusaders.

Near the port one of them, perhaps seven years old, is tugging at the arm of an American sailor, offering to find him a girl. Pulling away, the sailor, who is very drunk, slumps to the street. The urchin reaches for his wallet and the sailor pushes him away. Unable to roll his victim, the boy scurries off. In Naples the bigger boys pay urchins from 500 to 1,000 lire (80 cents to $1.60) for finding an American to beat up and strip of his cash, watch and clothes.

THERE are more than 10,000 of these homeless creatures, aged from six to 20, pimping, picking pockets, snatching purses, serving burglars as lookouts and smugglers as messengers, industrious and devious in the night as moles. They are called *scugnizzi*, from *scugnare*, which means "to spin like a top."

The *scugnizzi* have figured in Neapolitan folklore for more than three centuries. They flourished during World War II, when foreign soldiers filled the city. Many are the children of prostitutes, for Naples has many prostitutes and many passing sailors. But population growth and a dislocated economy have increased their numbers in Naples, and have produced a similar problem in Genoa, Palermo, Milan and other cities. In lean times they scrounge through garbage and eat fish heads. They swarm with vermin and are frequently diseased, and on cold nights they sneak into basements or seek out furnace gratings, on which they huddle together in the fetal position like savage little beasts.

Beasts? A remarkable young man, a Catholic priest, thought otherwise. Blond, blue-eyed Father Mario Borelli, son of a Neapolitan sheet-metal worker, was 28 years old in 1949 when he attacked the *scugnizzi* challenge head on. He got permission to use the bomb-blasted Church of the Mater Dei as a hostel. But the *scugnizzi*, he found, were no more interested in associating with a priest than with a policeman.

Courageous Father Borelli decided to go underground. He donned a tattered jacket and trousers and a dirty beret, and disappeared into the dangerous Neapolitan night. Being small (five feet, five inches) and cherub-faced, he had no trouble passing as a teen-aged *scugnizzo*.

For two winter months the priest had to give tacit approval to the boys' crimes. When they robbed drunks or indulged in immorality, he recalls, "I simply indicated indifference." On cold nights he huddled with them over the grates. When he had their confidence he began to pass an occasional word of the shelter in the old church. Late one February night he watched sadly as three of his companions rolled a drunk. "In five minutes they stripped him to the skin," says the priest. He plodded away, remarking wearily, "I'm going to Mater Dei to get out of the cold." The sullen trio followed him. After a night on cots and a hot breakfast, they returned to the street and passed the word to their friends.

A dozen *scugnizzi* showed up in the church with the shattered windows, then two dozen. By the winter's end there were 30, and they have come by the score ever since. Father Borelli gives the *scugnizzi* food and shelter first, but after that the most important thing is the restoration of their pride. "It takes long patient work, many talks and much understanding," he says, "to return a boy's self-respect."

The question of self-respect applies not only to the *scugnizzi* but to the entire country, and the two are not unconnected, for the *scugnizzi* are both a symptom and a result of Italy's problem. A country which destroys a child's self-respect because it no longer cares whether he is fed, clothed or loved has lost sight of one of the fundamentals of governing justly: respect for the individual. A nation which does not respect the most insignificant individual cannot respect itself.

ITALY came out of the last war crushed by the disillusionment of history. In its periods of glory it had twice been master of the West, once politically during the Roman era and once culturally during the Renaissance. But aside from these glories there were libertyless centuries of mortification, culminating in the double debasement of fascism and wartime defeat.

Because Italy had capitulated in 1943 and the partisan movement had assisted in its liberation, the country ended World War II considering itself one of the Allies. Self-pitying, the Italian people thought not of any possible guilt but of their suffering, and Benedetto Croce said, "Italy, formally defeated according to the laws of war and peace, does not feel defeated . . . but affirms its right to stand among the victors."

But the Allies—particularly the British— could not forget so quickly that the Italians had been partner to the Germans in their planned destruction. The peace treaty signed in 1947 was harsh. To the Italians, however, a blow fully as grievous was the country's exclusion from the United Nations for nearly a decade. Despite its wartime defeat, Italy had expected to be welcomed into the organization and thereby to regain its former status in world affairs. But its membership was blocked, first by war-weary Britain, France and Russia, and later by Russia alone as the Soviet Union bartered for the admission of its own satellite countries.

LICKING its wounds, Italy found a role for itself in the new security groups which were concerned with European affairs: the Council of Europe, the Western European Union and the North Atlantic Treaty Organization. It was one of the prime movers in the organization of the European Economic Community, or Common Market, the pan-European organization whose purpose is the reduction and eventual abolition of tariffs and other trade restrictions between member countries. In 1955, Italy was finally admitted to the U.N.

Though accepted on the international scene, Italy was still confronted with formidable internal ills. At the close of World War II the U.S. government had indicated that it was ready to aid in Italy's reconstruction, provided Italy adopted a government and an economic program of which it approved. Dependent upon the U.S. for economic survival, Italy went to the polls in 1948, in its first general election under the new constitution, and gave Premier Alcide De Gasperi's pro-American Christian Democrats a substantial majority. Soon thereafter the U.S. Marshall Plan and related programs gave Italy a tremendous boost toward economic well-being. But they did not essentially change the Italian economy, nor did they bring the country's historic problems closer to solution. These remain deeper and more complex than most Americans—and many Italians—realize.

Though the Christian Democrats have won popular support from the lower middle classes and the peasantry by promising bold social reforms, relatively few of these reforms have been enacted. They have been sidetracked within the party structure by self-preserving traditionalists who cling to the old rules and the old positions.

American financial and moral support of the Christian Democrats can be defended on the ground that there are no alternatives. In essence, Italians today must choose among three political groups: the neo-Fascists and the monarchists on the right, the Christian Democrats and allied parties in the center, and the Communists and Socialists on the left. With all their faults, the Christian Democrats are the only effective pro-western party.

But the Christian Democrats have done little to alter the basic economic structure of Italy, and that structure is a relic of history deliberately maintained to preserve those privileges which are also relics of history. The country's wealth is located mainly in the North and is controlled by a distinct minority: the industrialists, the landlords and the idle and still powerful aristocrats, many of whom channel their funds into investments abroad. While grants from the U.S. government have been pouring into Italy to provide working capital for Italian industrialists, and while this has increased employment and raised living standards among the lower middle classes and some of the lower classes, it has had little affect on the poorest people, for whom the funds were originally intended.

THE lack of progress is notable in other fields as well. The Italian bureaucracy is still composed to a large extent of men who made their careers under fascism. Newspaper proprietors who supported Mussolini still control powerful journals, and a few formerly Fascist professors occupy high university posts. Though the new constitution is a liberal one, the state is dominated by Roman Catholics who have little regard for political liberalism. The Church supports democratic precepts only when they protect or further its own position.

There is little doubt that in the increasing world-wide competition of political ideologies the Roman Catholic Church is one of the strongest spiritual forces against communism. However, there is evidence that in Italy, where men are simultaneously Catholics *and* Communists, the political influence of Catholicism may be overrated. Italy's reigning spirit is a "Catholic skepticism" which permits the people to live in the social atmosphere of the Church without accepting its dogma. The people maintain their saints and sanctuaries, their Catholic habits and instincts, but few of them pay much attention to the Church's political pronouncements.

There is a similar "political skepticism" in the average Italian's attitude toward communism. Certainly the presence of six million Communist voters is a constant menace to the country's political stability, but communism—Italian-style —is rooted in anticlerical protest and economic dissatisfaction rather than in the Soviet line. The popular attitude underlies a joke which one may hear in almost any Italian city.

Communist, boasting: "The Russians will invade Italy and arrest all anti-Communists."

Christian Democrat, boasting: "The Americans will invade Italy and arrest all Communists."

Innocent bystander: "*Madonna mia!* Who will be left?"

A second bystander: "The same forty-nine million Italians."

THE fact is that communism's appeal is no longer the mushrooming threat it once was. More than half the party's members are over 50 years of age, and only 10 per cent are between 20 and 30. What appears to be more significant is the postwar development of the neo-Fascist party called the Italian Social Movement (M.S.I.), which was organized by former supporters of Mussolini.

The crux of Italy's political problem is an immature and uninformed electorate. Here again much responsibility must rest with the Church. The maternal spirit of Italian Catholicism may be one of the causes of the carefree and affectionate human warmth which the world has always admired in Italy; but this spirit has also helped preserve the people's childlike irresponsibility toward public affairs.

Unless those who control Italy—the parliamentarians and the clerics, the landowners, the industrialists and the investors—undertake their own reforms, there will never be genuine reform in this aged land. The state must bear the burden of providing education to turn the masses into politically responsible citizens. The Church must help to build up a public opinion receptive to social change, to wean men away from a childish urge to be led and to give them the mature vision necessary for walking a man's road.

FATHER Borelli's way to save Italy is to save its children. He sees the *scugnizzi* as a product of all the ills of Italy—poverty, unemployment, lack of housing and schools—and a symbol of all the country's needs. At present the compassionate priest has 120 boys in two houses, the original church and an additional building opposite the Naples Cathedral. Because of his volcanic pace and his lavalike flow of words, Father Borelli is known as "Don Vesuvio." Sometimes he speaks in metaphors:

"An injustice done to one child is an injustice to the whole human family. The world is a body —no man is unaffected by what happens to another. No nation can live in health when there is infection in one corner of the world. The time has come when politicians must be humanitarians, or there will never be peace in the world."

The concept is not new in Italy, but by his practical application of it Father Borelli is pointing a way for his country. Italy's overriding problem, that of building a modern society and a viable state, must be solved from within. The country has the resources in its inexhaustible springs of vitality. Most people of the West carry life along with them like a burden. In Italy it is life that carries men with it like a flood, from one age to the next and into the future.

A worker descends an electrical tower near Messina. Next page: Homeless boys of Naples run with their benefactor, Father Borelli

NEW OPPORTUNITIES *for progress opened up by technical advances...*

. . . have if anything merely underlined the need for fresh approaches to the

150

ocial and educational problems that are the core of Italy's dilemma today

Appendix

HISTORICAL DATES

B.C.

11th Cent. Aeneas said to have landed in Italy

974-443 Greek colonies founded in Sicily and southern Italy

753 Traditional date for the mythical founding of Rome by Romulus

264-146 Rome, now supreme on Italian peninsula, enters Punic Wars and extends conquests abroad (Sicily, Greece, Carthage)

58-51 Caesar conquers Gaul, invades Britain

27 Empire declared under Augustus

A.D.

312-313 Constantine puts cross on his banners and wins Battle of Milvian Bridge. Christianity granted official toleration

330 Seat of empire moved to Constantinople (formerly called Byzantium). Empire is divided into East and West for administrative purposes

376-476 Invasions begin by Visigoths, Ostrogoths, Vandals and Huns

476 Rome taken by barbarians and sacked; end of Western Roman Empire

568 Lombards enter Italy from the north and overrun central areas of the country

754-800 Carolingians make alliance with popes, an agreement which culminates in Charlemagne's coronation as Emperor of revived Western Empire in 800

840 Moslems move into Sicily and southern Italy

11th to 14th Cents. Struggle for supremacy between popes and emperors; local disputes merging into this struggle take on the colors of Guelph and Ghibelline factions

Rise of the maritime republics (Amalfi, Pisa, Genoa, Venice); Italians dominate the Mediterranean Sea

Rise of the city-states (Florence, Milan, Ferrara, Siena) under strong leaders

1016-1091 Normans settle in the South and flourish

1220-1250 Swabian monarch Frederick II rules the South as Holy Roman Emperor; his court is a brilliant foretaste of the Renaissance

1309-1377 Papacy moves to Avignon in a "Babylonian captivity," marking a low ebb of Church's power. Even after popes return to Rome, feuds vitiate their influence, and no pope is strong again until 1447

1453 Fall of Constantinople to Islam, ending the Eastern Empire

1494 Lorenzo de' Medici dies; the monk Savonarola holds power in Florence until 1498

1494-1559 Age of invasions: Foreign powers, invited into Italy to lead factions, stay to dominate. Italy becomes a battleground on which France and Spain struggle for power

1559-1713 Spanish ascendancy in Italy (established by Emperor Charles V)

1701-1748 Wars of Spanish and Austrian Succession: Foreign powers fight over Italian territory

1748 Treaty of Aix-la-Chapelle confirms Austria as the owner of Lombardy and Venetia

1796 French invade Italy under Napoleon, introducing the ideals of the French Revolution into Italy

1802 Cisalpine Republic, founded by Napoleon in 1797, becomes the Italian Republic

1805 Napoleon crowned King of Italy; Austria loses its Italian possessions by treaty in 1806

1814 Napoleon overthrown; previous foreign powers move back into Lombardy-Venetia after Congress of Vienna in 1815

1815-1861 *Risorgimento*, a movement toward national unity and independence, gathers momentum under Mazzini, Cavour and Garibaldi

1831 Young Italy movement founded abroad by Mazzini. Insurrections in Italy

1848 Insurrections in Lombardy and Venice, supported by the King of Sardinia and by Pope Pius IX

1852 Cavour named prime minister in Piedmont

1859 War of Liberation. North Italian states (except Venetia and Trentino) incorporated into the Kingdom of Sardinia

1860 Garibaldi marches on Sicily, moving across to the mainland and advancing to Naples

Central Italian states annexed to the Kingdom of Sardinia

1861 First Italian parliament meets in Turin and proclaims the Kingdom of Italy, with Vittorio Emmanuele II as king

1866 Venetia ceded to Italy by Austria

1870 Triumphal entry of Italian troops into Rome—unification virtually completed. End of temporal power of papacy

1870-1915 Consolidation of the Italian kingdom under a parliamentary regime. Some colonial expansion (Eritrea, Tripoli, Somaliland; attempt at Ethiopia)

1882 Italy joins Austria and Germany in Triple Alliance

1915-1918 Italy joins Allies in World War I, declaring war on Austria in 1915, on Germany in 1916

1917 Collapse of the Italian front at Caporetto

1918-1922 Economic crisis; rise of the Fascist party

1919 D'Annunzio seizes Fiume; his action is disavowed by the Italian government

1922 Fascists march on Rome. With king's accord, Mussolini forms cabinet, is given dictatorial powers

1923-1924 Passage of Mussolini's electoral law; the minority of deputies left who are not Fascists leave the chamber, never to return

1929 Lateran Treaty creates an independent Vatican State and regulates relations between church and state

1935-1936 Conquest of Ethiopia, despite feeble sanctions by League of Nations

1936-1939 Fascist intervention in Spanish Civil War. German-Italian Alliance

1939 Italy takes Albania

1940 Italy joins Germany in war against France and Great Britain; against U. S. in 1941

1943 Allies land in Sicily. Mussolini is arrested and is succeeded by Badoglio, who signs surrender, declaring war on Germany

1945 All of Italy liberated by Allies with help of Italian army and partisan movement. Mussolini captured and killed by anti-Fascists

1946 Constituent Assembly. Republic of Italy is declared

1948 First elections won by Christian Democrats

1949 Italy joins NATO

1955 Italy enters the U. N.

1958 Elections: Government still in hands of center, dominated by Christian Democrats. Socialists gain

FOR FURTHER READING

CHAPTER 1: ITALY TODAY

Kubly, Herbert, *American in Italy*. Simon and Schuster, 1955.

Olschki, Leonardo, *The Genius of Italy*. Cornell University Press (reissue), 1954.

Prezzolini, Giuseppe, *The Legacy of Italy*. S. F. Vanni, 1948.

Sforza, Count Carlo, *Italy and the Italians*. E. P. Dutton and Company, Inc., 1949.

Wall, Bernard, *Italian Life and Landscape* (2 volumes). Paul Elek, 1950-1951.

CHAPTER 2: HISTORY (ROMAN EMPIRE AND THE RENAISSANCE)

Burckhardt, Jacob, *The Civilization of the Renaissance in Italy*. Available in several editions.

Durant, Will, *Caesar and Christ*. Simon and Schuster, 1944. *The Age of Faith*. Simon and Schuster, 1950. *The Renaissance*. Simon and Schuster, 1953.

Kantorowicz, Ernst, *Frederick the Second*. Frederick Ungar Publishing Co., 1957.

Lissner, Ivar, *The Caesars: Might and Madness*. G. P. Putnam's and Sons, 1958.

Lucas-Dubreton, J., *The Borgias*. E. P. Dutton & Co., Inc., 1955; Bantam Books, Inc., 1956.

Salvatorelli, Luigi, *A Concise History of Italy From Prehistoric Times to Our Own Day*. Oxford University Press, 1940.

Starr, Chester G., *Civilization and the Caesars; The Intellectual Revolution in the Roman Empire*. Cornell University Press, 1954.

Symonds, J. A., *The Renaissance in Italy*. Random House, Inc., 1935.

Winston, Richard, *Charlemagne, From the Hammer to the Cross*. Vintage Books, 1956.

Yourcenar, Marguerite, *Hadrian's Memoirs*. Farrar, Straus and Cudahy, 1954; Anchor Books, 1957.

CHAPTER 3: MODERN HISTORY AND POLITICS

Albrecht-Carrié, René, *Italy From Napoleon to Mussolini*. Columbia University Press, 1950.

Barr, Stringfellow, *Mazzini; Portrait of an Exile*. Henry Holt and Company, 1935.

Borgese, G. A., *Goliath; the March of Fascism*. The Viking Press, Inc., 1938.

Cesaresco, E. L. H. Martinengo, *Cavour*. Macmillan and Company, Ltd., London, 1898.

Croce, Benedetto, *A History of Italy, 1871-1915*. The Clarendon Press, Oxford, 1929.

Germino, Dante, *The Italian Fascist Party in Power; a Study of Totalitarian Rule*. University of Minnesota Press, 1959.

Mack Smith, Denis, *Cavour and Garibaldi, 1860*. Cambridge University Press, Cambridge, 1948. *Italy; a Modern History*. University of Michigan Press, 1959.

Matthews, Herbert L., *The Fruits of Fascism*. Harcourt, Brace and Company, 1943.

Mussolini, Benito, *My Autobiography*. Charles Scribner's Sons, 1928.

Salvemini, Gaetano, *Under the Axe of Fascism*. The Viking Press, Inc., 1936.

Trevelyan, G. M., *Garibaldi and the Thousand*. Longmans, Green and Co., 1928. *Garibaldi and the Making of Italy*. Longmans, Green and Co., 1928.

CHAPTER 4: THE NORTH

Greenfield, Kent Roberts, *Economics and Liberalism in the Risorgimento; A Study of Nationalism in Lombardy, 1814-1848*. Johns Hopkins Press, 1934.

Grindrod, Muriel, *The Rebuilding of Italy; Politics and Economics, 1945-55*. Oxford University Press, 1955.

Hughes, H. Stuart, *The United States and Italy*. Harvard University Press, 1953.

Kogan, Norman, *Italy and the Allies*. Harvard University Press, 1956.

Schmidt, Carl T., *The Plough and the Sword; Labor, Land and Property in Fascist Italy*. Columbia University Press, 1938.

Sturzo, Don Luigi, *Italy and the Coming World*. Roy Publishers, 1945.

CHAPTER 5: THE SOUTH

Dolci, Danilo, *Report From Palermo*. Orion Press, 1959.

Douglas, Norman, *Old Calabria*. Harcourt, Brace and Company, 1956. *Siren Land*. The Macmillan Company, 1957. *South Wind*. Random House, Inc., 1957.

Lawrence, D. H., *Sea and Sardinia*. Anchor Books, 1954.

Levi, Carlo, *Christ Stopped at Eboli*. Farrar, Straus and Cudahy, 1947. *Words Are Stones*. Farrar, Straus and Cudahy, 1958.

Silone, Ignazio, *Fontamara*. Atheneum Publishers, 1960. *Bread and Wine*. Harper & Brothers, 1937. *A Handful of Blackberries*. Harper & Brothers, 1953.

Vittorini, Elio, *In Sicily*. New Directions, 1949.

CHAPTER 6: WOMEN AND SOCIAL CHANGE

Bellonci, Maria, *The Life and Times of Lucrezia Borgia*. Harcourt, Brace and Company, 1953.

Lampedusa, Giuseppe di, *The Leopard*. Pantheon Publishers, 1960.

Wall, Bernard, *The Vatican Story*. Harper & Brothers, 1956.

West, Morris, *The Devil's Advocate*. William Morrow & Co., Inc., 1959.

CHAPTER 7: LEISURE

Berenson, Bernard, *The Passionate Sightseer*. Simon and Schuster, 1960.

Bowen, Elizabeth, *A Time in Rome*. Alfred A. Knopf, Inc., 1959.

Clark, Eleanor, *Rome and a Villa*. Doubleday & Company, Inc., 1952.

Fattorusso, Joseph, *Wonders of Italy*. G. Fattorusso, Florence, 1959.

McCarthy, Mary, *Stones of Florence*. Harcourt, Brace and Company, 1959. *Venice Observed*. Reynal & Company, 1956.

Morris, James, *The World of Venice*. Pantheon Books, Inc., 1960.

CHAPTER 8: LETTERS

Brooks, Van Wyck, *The Dream of Arcadia; American Writers and Artists in Italy, 1760-1913*. E. P. Dutton & Co., Inc., 1958.

De Sanctis, Francesco, *History of Italian Literature*. Basic Books, 1959.

Gaetani, Marguerite, editor, *New Italian Writers*. New Directions, 1950.

Highet, Gilbert, *Poets in a Landscape*. Alfred A. Knopf, Inc., 1957.

MacCurdy, Edward, editor, *The Notebooks of Leonardo da Vinci*. George Braziller, Inc., 1955.

Roeder, Ralph, *The Man of the Renaissance*. The Viking Press, Inc., 1933.

Wilkins, Ernest Hatch, *A History of Italian Literature*. Harvard University Press, 1954.

CHAPTER 9: ART AND MUSIC

Berenson, Bernard, *Italian Painters of the Renaissance*. Oxford University Press, 1930. Meridian Books, Inc., 1956.

Cellini, Benvenuto, *Autobiography*. Available in several editions.

Kidder-Smith, G. E., *Italy Builds; Its Modern Architecture and Native Inheritance*. Reinhold Publishing Corp., 1955.

Lang, Paul Henry, *Music in Western Civilization*. W. W. Norton & Company, Inc., 1941.

Newman, Ernest, *Great Operas* (2 volumes). Vintage Books, Inc., 1958.

Soby, James Thrall and Alfred H. Barr, Jr., *Twentieth Century Italian Art*. Museum of Modern Art, 1949.

Symonds, J. A., *The Life of Michelangelo*. Random House, Inc., 1959.

Toye, Francis, *Verdi; His Life and Works*. Alfred A. Knopf, 1946; Vintage Books, Inc., 1959.

Vasari, Giorgio, *The Lives of the Painters*. Available in several editions.

FAMOUS ITALIAN CULTURAL FIGURES AND THEIR PRINCIPAL WORKS

MUSIC

Landino, Francesco	13?? -1397	Blind organist and composer of Florence; his music a precursor of the Renaissance
Palestrina, Giovanni Pierluigi da	1525-1594	Liturgical music (Masses, motets): *Missa Papae Marcelli, Stabat Mater, Ecce Ego Joannes, Dum Complerentur*
Peri, Jacopo	1561-1633	Operas: *Dafne, Euridice*
Monteverdi, Claudio	1567-1643	Madrigals. Operas: *Orfeo (Orpheus), The Coronation of Poppaea*
Corelli, Arcangelo	1653-1713	Instrumental music: violin sonatas, concerti grossi
Scarlatti, Alessandro	1660-1725	Operas, cantatas. Important harmonic innovations
Vivaldi, Antonio	c.1675-1741	Concerti grossi: *The Four Seasons*. Operas (none now known). Influenced Bach
Scarlatti, Domenico	1685-1757	Important and original keyboard (harpsichord) sonatas. *Exercises*
Pergolesi, Giovanni Battista	1710-1736	Opera: *La Serva Padrona*. Chamber cantata: *Orpheus*. Church music: *Stabat Mater*
Boccherini, Luigi	1743-1805	Chamber works. Pioneer in history of stringed-instrument writing
Cherubini, Luigi	1760-1842	Operas: *Medea, The Water Carrier*. Church music
Paganini, Niccolò	1782-1840	Violin music (concertos and capriccios)
Rossini, Gioacchino Antonio	1792-1868	Operas: *L'Italiana in Algeri, The Barber of Seville, La Gazza Ladra, William Tell*
Donizetti, Gaetano	1797-1848	Operas: *Lucia di Lammermoor, Don Pasquale, The Daughter of the Regiment, La Favorita*
Bellini, Vincenzo	1801-1835	Operas: *Il Pirata, La Sonnambula, Norma, I Puritani*
Verdi, Giuseppe	1813-1901	Operas: *Nabucco, Ernani, Macbeth, La Traviata, Rigoletto, Il Trovatore, Un Ballo in Maschera, La Forza del Destino, Don Carlos, Aïda, Otello, Falstaff*. Also the *Manzoni Requiem*
Leoncavallo, Ruggiero	1858-1919	*I Pagliacci*
Puccini, Giacomo	1858-1924	Operas: *Manon Lescaut, La Bohème, Tosca, Turandot, Madama Butterfly*
Mascagni, Pietro	1863-1945	*Cavalleria Rusticana*
Malipiero, Gian Francesco	1882-	Operas, ballets, choral works, a string quartet and symphonic music. Revived Monteverdi
Respighi, Ottorino	1897-1936	Instrumental music: *The Fountains of Rome, The Pines of Rome, Feste Romane*. Operas
Dallapiccola, Luigi	1904-	Twelve-tone music. Settings of Greek lyrics. Operas: *Volo di Notte, Il Prigioniero, Job*

PAINTINGS

Cimabue, Giovanni	1240-1302	Moving from Byzantine manner to more natural one
Duccio di Buoninsegna	c.1255-1319	*Majestas*, Siena Cathedral. Possibly *Rucellai Madonna*. Byzantine concern with linear pattern, but more expressive
Giotto (di Bondone)	c.1266-1337	Frescoes in Assisi and Padua. Campanile of Florence Cathedral
Martini, Simone	c.1284-1344	*Majestas* fresco, Siena Palazzo Pubblico. Sant' Ansono *Annunciation*
Angelico, Fra (Giovanni da Fiesole)	1387-1455	Frescoes in San Marco convent, Florence; *Annunciation; Coronation of the Virgin*
Uccello, Paolo	1397-1475	Studies in perspective: frescoes. Scenes from Battle of San Romano
Masaccio (Tommaso Guidi)	1401-1428	Realistic perspective and lighting: frescoes in Santa Maria del Carmine, Florence
Lippi, Fra Filippo	c.1406-1469	Religious paintings: frescoes in Prato, *Coronation of the Virgin, Madonna* in profile
Francesca, Piero della	c.1420-1492	Monumental manner. True Cross frescoes, Arezzo; portrait of Federigo, Duke of Urbino
Bellini, Gentile	c.1429-1507	Crowd scenes with variety of face and incident: Holy Cross paintings in Venice
Bellini, Giovanni	c.1430-1516	Teacher of Giorgione and Titian. Serene, luminously colored paintings, altarpieces
Mantegna, Andrea	1431-1506	Concern with anatomy, perspective, design: *Holy Family, Triumph of Virtue, Parnassus*
Signorelli, Luca	c.1441-1523	Frescoes in Orvieto Cathedral. Strong treatment of nude bodies. Some pious works
Botticelli, Sandro	1444-1510	Lyrical line: *Birth of Venus, Primavera, Madonna of the Pomegranate, Calumny*
Ghirlandaio, Domenico	1449-1494	Frescoes: in Santa Maria Novella, life of St. Francis in Santa Trinità. Portraits within frescoes
Perugino (Pietro Vannucci)	c.1450-1524	Tender religious scenes: Cambio decorations, Perugia; Sistine Chapel frescoes
Vinci, Leonardo da	1452-1519	*Last Supper; Mona Lisa; The Virgin, St. Anne and the Infant Jesus; Madonna of the Rocks*
Carpaccio, Vittore	c.1455-1526	Series: *Legend of Saint Ursula, Life of St. George of the Slavonians*
Lippi, Filippino	c.1457-1504	Frescoes in Santa Maria Novella and in Santa Maria del Carmine
Michelangelo (Buonarroti)	1475-1564	Sistine Chapel ceiling
Giorgione (da Castelfranco)	c.1477-1510	Fusion of forms, pervading tonality: *Fête Champêtre, Sleeping Venus*
Titian (Tiziano Vecelli)	1477-1576	Voluptuous color and beauty: *Sacred and Profane Love, Venus and Adonis*
Raphael (Raffaello Sanzio)	1483-1520	Classical religious paintings: *Sistine Madonna, Marriage of the Virgin, School of Athens*
del Sarto, Andrea	1486-1531	Rich color: *Holy Family, Madonna of the Harpies*
Correggio (Antonio Allegri)	1494-1534	Experiments in foreshortening, splendid bodies: *Rape of Ganymede, Leda and the Swan*
Tintoretto (Jacopo Robusti)	1518-1594	Dramatic paintings: decorations in Venice, *Bacchus and Ariadne*
Veronese (Paolo Caliari)	1528-1588	Decorative paintings of Venetian opulence, *The Rape of Europa, The Marriage of Cana*
Caravaggio, Michelangelo Amerighi da	c.1573-1609	Founder of realism in Rome; dramatic light and shade
Tiepolo, Giovanni Battista	c.1696-1770	Decorative, theatrical, with great space and airy color: frescoes in Doges' and Labio Palaces
Canaletto (Antonio Canale)	1697-1768	Cityscapes, especially scenes of Venice
Guardi, Francesco	1712-1793	Venetian landscapes with almost impressionistic play of light
Carrà, Giacomo	1881-	Futurist and metaphysical paintings: *Funeral of the Anarchist Galli, The Tram*
Chirico, Giorgio de	1888-	Strangely still, ominous world of hard light and geometric shapes: "piazzas of Italy"
Morandi, Giorgio	1890-	Poetic treatment of forms in still life. Bottles, molded forms in muted tones
Campigli, Massimo	1895-	Figure paintings of archaic elegance and portraits
Afro (Basaldella)	1912-	Romantic development from roots of later Picasso

SCULPTURE AND ARCHITECTURE

Brunelleschi, Filippo	1377-1446	Architecture: Pitti Palace, octagonal dome of Florence Cathedral
Ghiberti, Lorenzo	1378-1455	Sculpture: bronze relief doors on Florence Baptistery
Donatello (Donato di Niccolò di Betto Bardi)	1386-1466	Sculpture: Crucifixion, David, equestrian Gattamelata
Della Robbia, Luca	1400-1482	Sculpture in terra cotta. Decorations in Florence Duomo
Verrocchio, Andrea del	1435-1488	Sculpture: Christ and Doubting Thomas, Boy With Dolphin, equestrian Colleoni
Bramante (Donato d'Agnolo)	1444-1514	Belvedere, at the Vatican. Plan for Via Giulia
Michelangelo (Buonarroti)	1475-1564	Sculpture: David, *Pietà*, Moses. Designed Medici Chapel, Dome of St. Peter's
Palladio, Andrea	1518-1580	Revival of ancient architectural Roman style: Basilica and Olympic Theater, Vicenza
Bernini, Giovanni Lorenzo	1598-1680	Baroque sculpture and architecture: Colonnade at St. Peter's, Vatican Royal Stairway
Nervi, Pier Luigi	1891-	Engineering: Exhibition Halls, Turin; Sports Palace, Rome
Ponti, Gio	1891-	Architecture: Pirelli Rubber and Montecatini Buildings in Milan
Marini, Marino	1901-	Sculpture: large-scale figure pieces, portraits
Manzù, Giacomo	1908-	Sculpture: tender figures of women and adolescents
Mirko (Basaldella)	1910-	Abstract sculpture, often with detailed surfaces

LITERATURE

Cicero, M. Tullius	106-43 B.C.	Speeches and letters; transmitter of Greek thought to Middle Ages
Caesar, G. Julius	100-44	*Commentaries.* Simplicity in prose style
Catullus, G. Valerius	84-54	Intensely personal lyric poetry of love and bitterness
Vergil (P. Vergilius Maro)	70-19	Nationalistic and idealistic poetry: *The Aeneid, The Georgics, The Eclogues*
Horace (Q. Horatius Flaccus)	68-8	Lyrics, as well as poetry of life and manners of his time: *Satires, Odes, Epistles*
Ovid (P. Ovidius Naso)	43 B.C.-18 A.D.	Elegiac poetry of pleasure and eroticism: *The Art of Love, Metamorphoses*
Seneca, Lucius Annaeus	1-65 A.D.	Statesman, Stoic philosopher and dramatist
Petronius, Gaius	?-66	Fragment of prose novel, *The Satyricon* of Petronius Arbiter
Tacitus, Cornelius	54-119	History: *Annals, Histories*
Suetonius (G. Suetonius Tranquillus)	2nd Century	Biography: *Lives of the Twelve Caesars*
Polo, Marco	c.1250-1324	Traveler. *The Description of the World*
Dante (Dante Alighieri)	1265-1321	Poetry: *The Divine Comedy.* Treatise: *De Monarchia*
Petrarch (Francesco Petrarca)	1304-1374	Italian and Latin lyrics, love poems: *Canzoniere.* Latin treatises
Boccaccio, Giovanni	1313-1375	Tales: *The Decameron*
Macchiavelli, Niccolò	1469-1527	Statesman and political writer: *The Prince. Mandragola*, a comedy
Ariosto, Lodovico	1474-1533	Poetry: *Orlando Furioso*
Castiglione, Baldassare	1478-1529	Statesman and author. *The Book of the Courtier*
Guicciardini, Francesco	1483-1540	History: *Political and Civil Reminiscences, Florentine History, History of Italy*
Aretino, Pietro	1492-1556	Dramatist, wit, satirist. Plays: *The Horatii.* Letters, lyrics, pious Lives
Cellini, Benvenuto	1500-1571	Autobiography: *The Life of Benvenuto Cellini*
Tasso, Torquato	1544-1595	Poetry: *Aminta, Jerusalem Delivered*
Galilei, Galileo	1564-1642	Astronomer, mathematician, physicist. *Dialogues Concerning Two New Sciences*
Vico, Giovanni Battista	1668-1744	Philosophy: *On the One Principle and One End of Universal Law, Principles of a New Science*
Goldoni, Carlo	1707-1793	Dramas: *La Locandiera, Women's Gossip, The Tyrants, Quarrels at Chioggia*
Gozzi, Carlo	1720-1806	Dramas: *Il Corvo, Turandot, The Love for Three Oranges*
Alfieri, Vittorio	1749-1803	Poetry and dramas: *Maria Stuart, Life of Philip the Second, Myrrha, Saul*
Manzoni, Alessandro	1785-1873	Tragedies, poetry. Novel: *I Promessi Sposi (The Betrothed)*
Leopardi, Giacomo	1798-1837	Poetry: *Song to Italy, The Dominant Thought, The Village Saturday Evening.* Prose: *Little Moral Pieces*
Carducci, Giosuè	1835-1907	Poetry: *Hymn to Satan, Barbarian Odes, Rhymes and Rhythms*
Verga, Giovanni	1840-1922	Novels: *Cavalleria Rusticana, The House by the Medlar Tree.* Established *verismo* (realism)
Svevo, Italo	1861-1928	Novels: *Confessions of Zeno, As a Man Grows Older*
D'Annunzio, Gabriele	1863-1938	Poetry and novels: *Pleasure, The Dead City, Fire.* Dramatic poem: *The Daughter of Jorio*
Croce, Benedetto	1866-1952	Philosophy and criticism: *The Philosophy of the Spirit; History as the Story of Liberty*
Pirandello, Luigi	1867-1936	Dramas: *Six Characters in Search of an Author, As You Desire Me.* Short stories
Deledda, Grazia	1871-1930	Novels: *Elias Portolu, The Faults of Others, The Mother*
Ungaretti, Giuseppe	1888-	Poetry: *Joy, Grief, The Feeling of Time, Life of a Man*
Betti, Ugo	1892-1953	Dramas: *Goat Island, The Gambler*
Montale, Eugenio	1896-	Poetry: *Finisterre, Cuttlefish Bones, Le Occasione*
Malaparte, Curzio	1898-1957	Political writings, short stories: *Sodom and Gomorrah, Kaputt*
Silone, Ignazio	1900-	Novels: *Fontamara, Bread and Wine, The Secret of Luca*
Quasimodo, Salvatore	1901-	Poetry, classical translations
Levi, Carlo	1902-	Narrative reports: *Christ Stopped at Eboli, Words Are Stones*
Moravia, Alberto	1907-	Novels: *The Woman of Rome, Two Women, Bitter Honeymoon, Two Adolescents*
Pavese, Cesare	1908-1950	Novels: *The Moon and the Bonfires, Before the Cock Crows*
Vittorini, Elio	1908-	Novels: *In Sicily, The Twilight of the Elephant, The Red Carnation*
Morante, Elsa	1918-	Novels: *Arturo's Island, The House of Liars*
Calvino, Italo	1923-	Fables, novels: *The Baron in the Trees, The Path to the Nest of Spiders*

Credits

The sources for the illustrations in this book are shown below. Credits for pictures from left to right are separated by commas, top to bottom by dashes.

AN ACKNOWLEDGMENT

The editors of this book are particularly indebted to Shepard B. Clough, Professor of History, Columbia University, who read and commented in detail on the entire text.

Index

Printed and bound by R. R. Donnelley & Sons Company
Chicago, Illinois, and Crawfordsville, Indiana